Microfinance

As microfinance is increasingly being absorbed into broader debates on financial inclusion and sustainable development, there is a growing number of professionals operating in international relations and development who are often confronted with sweeping statements about the alleged benefits and risks of microfinance. This book provides a concise introduction to microfinance – the key issues, debates, research agenda and public policy relevance.

Illustrated by real-life examples, the book's sections also highlight key publications and data sources and identify gaps for future research. The book will be an invaluable resource both for development economists and for scholars in neighbouring disciplines who need to get up to speed quickly on the current debates and research in microfinance.

Bernd Balkenhol is Professor for Microfinance and Financial Inclusion at the University of Geneva (Geneva School of Economics and Management). He is former Director of the Social Finance Program at the International Labor Organization (ILO) and senior policy advisor to the Central Bank of West African States (BCEAO) in Dakar. He represented ILO at CGAP and the G20 Global Partnership for Financial Inclusion, and coordinated the IV European Microfinance Research Conference in 2015 at the University of Geneva. He acquired his PhD at the University of Freiburg and an MA at the Fletcher School of Law and Diplomacy (Medford, Mass.).

Routledge Focus on Economics and Finance

The fields of economics are constantly expanding and evolving. This growth presents challenges for readers trying to keep up with the latest important insights. Routledge Focus on Economics and Finance presents short books on the latest big topics, linking in with the most cutting-edge economics research.

Individually, each title in the series provides coverage of a key academic topic, whilst collectively the series forms a comprehensive collection across the whole spectrum of economics.

Cash, Corruption and Economic Development
Vikram Vashisht

The Essentials of M&A Due Diligence
Peter Howson

Cities, Economic Inequality and Justice
Reflections and Alternative Perspectives
Edwin Buitelaar, Anet Weterings and Roderik Ponds

Reinventing Accounting and Finance Education
For a Caring, Inclusive and Sustainable Planet
Atul Shah

Microfinance
Research, Debates, Policy
Bernd Balkenhol

For a full list of titles in this series, please visit https://www.routledge.com/Routledge-Focus-on-Economics-and-Finance/book-series/RFEF

Microfinance
Research, Debates, Policy

Bernd Balkenhol

LONDON AND NEW YORK

First published 2018
by Routledge
2 Park Square, Milton Park, Abingdon, Oxon OX14 4RN

and by Routledge
711 Third Avenue, New York, NY 10017

Routledge is an imprint of the Taylor & Francis Group, an informa business

© 2018 Bernd Balkenhol

The right of Bernd Balkenhol to be identified as author of this work has been asserted by him in accordance with sections 77 and 78 of the Copyright, Designs and Patents Act 1988.

All rights reserved. No part of this book may be reprinted or reproduced or utilised in any form or by any electronic, mechanical, or other means, now known or hereafter invented, including photocopying and recording, or in any information storage or retrieval system, without permission in writing from the publishers.

Trademark notice: Product or corporate names may be trademarks or registered trademarks, and are used only for identification and explanation without intent to infringe.

British Library Cataloguing-in-Publication Data
A catalogue record for this book is available from the British Library

Library of Congress Cataloging-in-Publication Data
Names: Balkenhol, Bernd, author.
Title: Microfinance: research, debates, policy / Bernd Balkenhol.
Description: 1st Edition. | New York: Routledge, 2018. |
Series: Routledge focus on economics and finance |
Includes bibliographical references and index.
Identifiers: LCCN 2018007751 |
ISBN 9781138732803 (hardback) | ISBN 9781315187976 (ebook)
Subjects: LCSH: Microfinance.
Classification: LCC HG178.3 B375 2018 | DDC 332.7—dc23
LC record available at https://lccn.loc.gov/2018007751

ISBN: 978-1-138-73280-3 (hbk)
ISBN: 978-1-315-18797-6 (ebk)

Typeset in Times New Roman
by codeMantra

To Anna, Mathias and Sebastian.
To Regula.

Contents

List of figures	ix
List of tables	x
Preface	xi
Acknowledgements	xii
List of Acronyms	xiii

1 Microfinance: common views and preconceived ideas	1
2 Microfinance: a response to market failure	7
3 The demand for microfinance	15
4 Products and services	21
5 Methods and techniques	31
6 Microfinance institutions	41
7 Investing in microfinance	62
8 Subsidies	70
9 Microfinance markets	77

viii *Contents*

10	Public policy	87
11	Impact	109
12	What next?	122
	References	129
	Index	141

Figures

2.1	Financial transactions: simplistic view	7
2.2	Financial transactions with transaction costs	8
6.1	Scatter gram: scores and clusters	57
6.2	Best practice frontier in two output coordinates	58
6.3	Best practice frontier in two input coordinates	58
7.1	Types of investors and types of funds	63
7.2	Return expectations of investors in microfinance	66
7.3	Social performance of MFIs with MIV investments	68
9.1	Global Interest Yield Trends in microfinance 2004–2011	80
9.2	Evolution of interest rates of banks and MFIs (Bolivia 1992–2007)	81
9.3	Components of interest yields in microfinance 2004–2011	82
10.1	Sources of debt financing, sub-Sahara Africa 2011	100
10.2	Average interest rate on credit lines to MFIs (weighted average, sub-Sahara Africa)	101
11.1	The impact of microcredit: findings of six randomised control trials	114
12.1	Mobile money account penetration in sub-Saharan Africa	124

Tables

2.1	Interest rates compared: banks, MFIs and the informal financial sector (annual percentage rates)	11
4.1	The legal form largely determines the liabilities structure	23
5.1	Poverty targeting strategies by selected African MFIs	32
5.2	Targeting and the implications for expenses and yields	33
5.3	Group versus individual lending: cost implications	35
5.4	Property registries in Tanzania	37
6.1	Microfinance institutions worldwide (MFIs on the MIX Market)	42
6.2	Features of different types of MFIs	43
6.3	Indicators of financial and social performance by type of MFI	45
6.4	Financial performance of MFIs by charter type (2009–2016)	46
6.5	Transformation: implications for funding costs and overheads	53
8.1	Efficiency and profitability in Latin American MFIs	73
9.1	Microfinance market penetration 2009	78
9.2	Market concentration (active borrower accounts Bangladesh 2009)	79
9.3	Mission drift? Average loan amounts/GDP per head (%) of selected Latin American MFIs 1990–2006	84
10.1	Top 10 wholesale funds (Apexes) 2009	102
12.1	Microfinance in impact investment portfolios	125

Preface

Why another book on microfinance?

The time just seems right: after the first decade of hype and a second decade of criticism, microfinance largely disappeared from the headlines. The right time for a balanced presentation. There have been fresh debates in the past few years about impact, the role of government, subsidies, digital finance and the place of microfinance in impact investing: good enough reasons to explore how these issues hang together.

This book is meant as an introduction to the field of microfinance, intended for a public interested in development issues in general and first year students in economics and social sciences.

The aim is to provide a succinct overview of the main issues in research and policy. It is not intended as a systematic encyclopaedic treatise.

The reader is hopefully inspired to explore specific aspects of microfinance in greater depth.

The book is based on a Master level course at the University of Geneva.

Acknowledgements

Many individuals contributed to this book through questions, interrogations and criticism. It would be impossible to name them individually.

For the lively and inspiring exchanges over the years, I wish to thank my colleagues and friends in the ILO's Social Finance Program.

I benefitted from debates at the research conferences organized by the European Microfinance Platform. I appreciated these opportunities to learn, exchange and discover.

Much of what I learnt about microfinance goes back to exchanges and discussions at CGAP meetings, which were occasions to question standard views and preconceived notions about microfinance.

I am grateful to Yves Flückiger and Marcelo Olarreaga, respectively Rector of the University of Geneva and Dean of the Geneva School of Economics and Management, for their support and encouragement.

My views of microfinance were shaped and influenced by Jonathan Morduch. Without his inspiration, this book could not have been written.

Acronyms

Apex	Wholesale fund
ASCA	Accumulating savings and credit association
CGAP	Consultative Group to Assist the Poor (donor consortium based at the World Bank)
DFI	Development Finance Institution
FCFA	Franc CFA (currency of the West African Economic and Monetary Union)
FSS	Financial self-sufficiency, a measure of profitability
G2P	Government to Persons (payments like allowances and pensions)
GNI	Gross National Income
IFC	International Finance Corporation
ILO	International Labour Organization
IPO	Initial Public Offering
MBB	Micro Banking Bulletin
MENA	Middle East and North Africa
MFI	Microfinance Institution
MIV	Microfinance Investment Vehicle
MIX	Market Data base with information on over 2000 MFIs
MNO	Mobile Network Operator
NBFI	Non-Bank Financial Institution
NGO	Non-Governmental Organization
OSS	Operational self-sufficiency, a measure of profitability
RCT	Randomized Control Trial (experimental evaluation technique)
RoA	Return on Assets, a measure of profitability
RoE	Return on Equity, a measure of profitability
ROSCA	Rotating Savings and Credit Association
SDGs	Sustainable Development Goals
SME	Small and Medium Enterprise
UNDP	United Nations Development Program

1 Microfinance
Common views and preconceived ideas

If only poverty could be wiped out, rapidly, massively, once and for all and without redistribution and constraints, without political and social upheaval, simply by giving the poor the financial means to work themselves out of poverty! This wish appears unrealistic, but this is exactly what advocates of microfinance have claimed since the late 1980s: provide finance in small amounts to people without assets and without a track record so that they can work themselves out of poverty. An enormous task on its own right, but what microfinance proponents promised in addition seemed even less plausible: that there was a business case in microfinance, that it was possible to build self-financing, even profitable institutions. The message of microfinance was simple: there are opportunities for income generation even in the most destitute slum; there are also ways to give the poor the means to protect their livelihoods against the most severe shocks. Funding on the right terms would empower the poor and kick off a beneficial cycle stabilising or even lifting incomes and welfare – and do it as a business.

The consecration came in 2006, when Yunus and the Grameen Bank were awarded the Nobel Peace prize for their *"efforts to create economic and social development from below."*[1] Microcredit was recognised and lauded as a *"means to break out of poverty."* The simple message seemed to have caught on. *The New York Times*, *The Wall Street Journal*, the *Economist* and other global media jumped on the bandwagon and published op-eds on the merits of microfinance. With over two billion people living on less than $2 a day, just waiting to be reached by microfinance institutions, microfinance looked set on a dramatic growth trajectory for many years to come.

At the same time, global networks promoting microfinance spread success stories of clients who had made it. The language used in aid circles (*"best"* practice) revealed a sense of absolute certainty about what was good for the poor, for the institution, for markets and policy.

2 Microfinance: common views

Another term often used at that time, *"the bottom of the pyramid,"*[2] suggested that far from questioning the existing social and economic order, microfinance was key to opening up commercial opportunities in the vast segment of people living on less than $2 a day. Far from turning the pyramid upside down, microfinance seemed to be content to exploit social business opportunities.

But before long the field of microfinance encountered several fundamental challenges. In some markets, microfinance had become too successful for its own good: excessively high interest rates, portfolio growth based on aggressive peddling of microloans and disregard for the risks of over-indebtedness of poor client households. The IPOs of Compartamos[3] in Mexico in 2007 and of SKS in India in 2008[4] raised the question how much commercialisation was good for the field and whether it was about to lose sight of its social mission. The second challenge was politics. Microfinance promoters began to realize that they had stepped onto a minefield of political and social sensitivities: poverty is, after all, a social and political issue. It touched at the legitimacy of established public welfare institutions. Keen not to be outdone by foreign-sponsored NGOs, some governments launched their own microfinance institutions.

The clash was inevitable: in 2009–2010 the State Government of Andhra Pradesh in India blamed reported cases of suicides by over-indebted farmers on microfinance institutions. The full evidence has not been established, but the damage was done.[5] The State Government of Andhra Pradesh encouraged customers of microfinance institutions to default on their loans, thereby accelerating a massive and systematic degradation of the portfolio of microfinance institutions in that State, driving several into insolvency and damaging the reputation of the entire sector. Critics of microfinance picked on this incident to argue generally that the poor would have been better off had they refrained from contracting small loans. It would have been more effective to change the distribution of incomes through social and fiscal policies and address directly the causes of vulnerability.

Communications in the media by both advocates and opponents shaped the perceptions of microfinance. Messages in the public domain tend to be simplistic – and continue to be so.[6] In reality there are thousands of microfinance institutions in over 120 countries, differing in size, type, performance and business model. In such a heterogeneous field it would make more sense to differentiate and qualify – but this is not the material for headlines. There are no simple answers to questions like whether there are real net benefits to the poor, whether microfinance institutions are genuine social enterprises and whether societies on the

Microfinance: common views 3

whole are better off with microfinance or without. Reality is more complicated. There are numerous factors that need to be taken into account before attempting to answer any of these questions: the institution itself, how it is funded and set up legally, the nature of demand by households and enterprises in local financial markets, policies and regulations that provide the framework for the activities of microfinance institutions. Yes, there have been some outstanding success stories in microfinance, as there have been a few failures, while the vast majority of institutions display a moderately impressive track record. If one wants to find out what really makes up microfinance, then it helps to look not only at the stars and laggards, but above all the average performers.

After all, for all the hype[7] and crises of the past years, microfinance is still around. It seems to respond to a real need. It surely is not just a fashion in development. One explanation is that it can indeed be profitable to distribute financial services on a very small scale to poor people, under certain conditions. If all microfinance institutions were loss-makers, or if they ceased to interact with the poor, then microfinance would be of no interest. What continues to appeal is the double bottom line in microfinance, i.e. the proposition to reduce and eradicate poverty by commercial means. Facts and figures on outreach to the poor[8] appear to support the promise of microfinance. Thousands of microfinance institutions (MFIs) worldwide start up and grow, some stagnate and a few fail and disappear. Some are innovative and design new products remaining close to the demand of poor households and very small enterprises, while others just prod along doing the same things year in, year out.

Far from fading away, microfinance even withstood and survived several crises. Moreover, the intriguing double bottom line of microfinance has started to influence mainstream trends in the financial sector, like responsible finance, sustainable finance and impact investing. These take their cue from microfinance,[9] its values, language and the tools to track impact on clients.

And despite crises and controversies, microfinance as a field continues to fascinate researchers who struggle to find answers to questions like:

- How can it be that financial institutions succeed commercially with portfolios of small transactions?
- Why do poor households pay seemingly exorbitant interest rates?
- How far has competition brought down interest rates?
- Do MFIs lose sight of their social mission over time and with increasing commercialisation?

4 *Microfinance: common views*

- Is there a trade-off between financial performance and impact on the poor?
- Are the poor really better off because of microfinance?

Before taking up these questions in the following chapters it may help to clear up a number of misconceptions that stem from the way the field of microfinance has evolved. One microfinance institution in particular shaped the ideas in the general public, Grameen Bank. Microfinance as practiced by Grameen Bank and similar institutions in South Asia meant: microcredit – and not any other financial service; it meant catering to poor women organised in joint liability groups – and not individual men or individual women above the cut-off poverty line; and it meant loans earmarked for income generation and microenterprises – and not for any other purpose. The typical microfinance client was a woman organised in a solidarity group.

Gradually other approaches evolved, making the field more heterogeneous: promoted by ACCION and Opportunity International, two international NGOs, microfinance institutions in Latin America sprang up that focused more on the individual micro-entrepreneur client. Since then, more business models sprung up in microfinance, ranging from cooperatives, to non-banking financial institutions and subsidiaries of commercial banks, all claiming a double bottom line. Over the following decades microfinance as a field has grown in volume, numbers and diversity, making the initial simplistic views of microfinance obsolete.

Even before *modern* microfinance started in the late 1970s, there have been initiatives to bring about improvements in the lives for the poor through access to finance. The term "microfinance" may be new, but there are historic precedents of practices that could be labelled *historic* microfinance. Pawnshops, thrift societies, savings and credit cooperatives are precursors of modern microfinance and occasionally exist side by side with modern microfinance institutions. Savings and credit cooperatives express the commitment of farmers, artisans, craftsmen and others to help themselves, while thrift societies and municipal pawn shops are the result of public initiatives. All three types of historic microfinance institutions have in common the aim to avoid or reduce over-indebtedness of the poor.[10]

What emerges is a unique set of features that may explain why microfinance has survived and why it is likely to be around, for years to come as an object of research and a field for development economics. It is hard to pigeonhole it as a discipline: is it social development? A subset of financial sector development? Part of economic development? Whatever its classification, microfinance has features that explain its robustness, global presence and adaptability to various circumstances:

- the resources are largely mobilised and recycled locally;
- microfinance succeeds in building solid, viable institutions that grow and innovate;[11]
- some of these institutions are doing so well that they attract outside investors, social and commercial;
- above all, microfinance gives choice. It treats the client as a sovereign actor and informed market participant, capable of making responsible decisions on finance for consumption, investment and savings. If poverty is lack of opportunities (A. Sen), then microfinance may hold the key to end poverty.

Notes

1 www.nobelprize.org/nobel_prizes/peace/laureates/2006/.
2 C.K. Prahalad, *The Fortune at the Bottom of the Pyramid.* Wharton School Publication, 2004.
3 R. Rosenberg, Reflections on the Compartamos initial public offering: a case study on microfinance interest rates and profits, CGAP Focus Note 42, June 2007.
4 G. Chen et al., Indian Microfinance Goes Public: The SKS Initial Public Offering, CGAP Focus Note 65, September 2010.
5 CGAP, Andhra Pradesh 2010: Global Implications of the Crisis in Indian Microfinance, Focus Note 67, November 2010.
6 See for example the website of the International Year of Microcredit 2005.
7 Thomas Dichter, Hype and Hope: The worrisome state of the microcredit movement, Blog on Microfinance Gateway, CGAP 2006.
8 www.themix.org
9 See presentation by the SPTF at the GIIN Investor Forum December 2016 in Amsterdam (also: https://thegiin.org/assets/IRIS%20SPTF%20and%20 the%20Investor%20Perspective_vFINAL.pdf).
10 In the middle of the 19th century, Friedrich Wilhelm Raiffeisen, mayor of a small locality in Germany, encouraged small farmers to organise themselves in self-help societies for the collection of savings and lending. His initiative was set against the backdrop of widespread over-indebtedness of small farmers at the hand of trader-usurers in livestock and cereals. In the 19th century no one spoke of "microfinance," but the aims, products, strategies and operations of these institutional precursors were not much different from present-day microfinance institutions. Already in the late 18th century city administrations in Europe set up thrift societies to ease the financial burden of the urban poor. These were meant as accessible alternatives to the usurer. One of the first thrift societies was established in Hamburg in 1778, followed by the first communal savings fund ("Sparkasse") in 1801. These "historic" microfinance institutions have done quite well, survived the past 160 years and are now the banking partner of

6 *Microfinance: common views*

choice for most small and medium enterprises in many European countries. Municipal pawnshops are even older. In the late middle ages several Italian towns set up pawnshops (Monte Pietà) with the aim to give the poor access to small loans at zero or very low interest. Again, the intention was to give the poor an affordable alternative to the usurer. (See also: H.D. Seibel, History matters in Microfinance, *Small Enterprise Development*, vol. 14, no. 2, June 2003; D. Steinwand, *The Alchemy of Microfinance*. Berlin, Verlag für Wissenschaft und Forschung, 2001; J.D. Von Pischke, *Finance at the Frontier*. Washington DC, The World Bank, 1991.)

11 R. Cull, A. Demirguc-Kunt and J. Morduch, The Microfinance Business Model – Enduring Subsidy and Modest Profit, Policy Research Working Paper 7786, World Bank Development Research Group, August 2016.

2 Microfinance
A response to market failure

There would be no need for microfinance if banks catered to individual clients whatever the amounts and in the absence of security: land, machines or buildings. In a market with full transparency and perfect information among all contracting parties, it would not make a difference that clients are not easily identifiable or that they lacked a tax and social security number. In a perfect market, there would also be no need for loan appraisals and other bank-internal reviews. With full transparency, financial contracts could be concluded at zero transaction costs: the price paid for a loan by a borrower (i.e. the interest rate i) would be identical to r, the yield obtained by the lender (Figure 2.1).

However, in real-life financial markets there is no complete transparency. Market actors tend to withhold information from their contracting partners. This is especially the case with clients who live and work

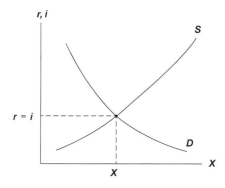

Figure 2.1 Financial transactions: simplistic view.

8 Microfinance: a response to market failure

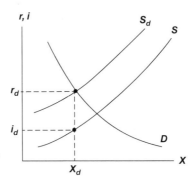

Figure 2.2 Financial transactions with transaction costs.

in the informal economy – as in most low-income countries. Banks have to undertake enquiries to find out what the prospective client is really up to and to size up the risk of default. Generating risk-related information entails costs to market actors, "transaction costs." The bank charges these costs on top of the interest rate, so as to preserve its net benefit. In contrast to the perfect market scenario, the client will now see the interest rate topped by a premium representing these transaction costs: r is no longer identical with i, loans become scarcer and more expensive (Figure 2.2).

One could argue that commercial banks could nevertheless attempt to appraise the default risks of clients in the smaller, informal and least transparent market segments as long as they could charge the costs incurred to the borrower. However, this is unlikely for three practical reasons:

- The owners of banks expect returns on their investments; if a bank engaged in many small loan transactions although the alternative is feasible, namely to engage in a few large size transactions, then shareholders would not be satisfied. The governance and business model in commercial banking thus discourage smaller transactions.
- Financial transactions by established formal financial institutions carry a substantial share of fixed costs; the larger the institution, the more this is so. Whether a loan is for $200 or for $20,000, the staff time required for appraisal and administrative overheads remains the same. Everything else being equal, larger transactions produce higher yields to the bank. Since larger transactions produce higher yields to the bank, it tends to prefer larger transactions.

Microfinance: a response to market failure 9

- There is always an element of risk in lending. To protect against the risk of default, banks make sure to obtain some rights over assets owned by the client. That is not possible in situations where the client has no assets nor even a registered identity. Alternatively banks could factor into the interest rate a substantial margin to protect against an eventual default. However, even that is not a full proof security. Very high interest rates may attract the "wrong" kind of clients, namely those who expect to generate very high returns on their investment, in other words above-average risk-takers.

Economic theory[1] has developed tools to explain the causes of lacking transparency, especially in financial contracts:

- ... "information asymmetry," i.e. when lenders do not have full information about the borrower's capacity or willingness to pay back; this applies generally to financial contracts, but even more so when one of the parties is undocumented.
- "moral hazard," when clients reckon that they can get away with default; this has been observed, for example, in microloan programmes that were funded by the government. Clients who know that they owe money ultimately to the government are more likely to default.
- "adverse selection," a consequence of information asymmetry, occurs for example in situations where the demand for micro health insurance is highest by those most likely to fall ill or to suffer accidents.
- "principal – agent" issues, another outcome of information asymmetry; in this case it is in the relation between an individual ("agent") mandated by another individual ("principal") to act and take decisions on his behalf, yet pursuing his own agenda; an example is the relation between managers of a cooperative and cooperative members.

These aspects of market failure in financial intermediation explain why private commercial banks appear ill-suited to engage with the millions of household-enterprises in the informal economy. Imagine a transaction between a street vendor in Lagos and the National Commercial Bank of Nigeria. The information asymmetry is multiple and complex. It goes both ways: the bank is unable to screen the realistic default risk of such an informal potential client, while the street vendor has no clue how to approach, speak to and negotiate with the bank. In fact, millions of "household-enterprises" in low income countries would not even consider

10 *Microfinance: a response to market failure*

banks as possible funding sources. Yet, they do occasionally need external funding. Since modern microfinance has been around for only the last 40 years, one wonders what "household-enterprises" did before.

The informal real economy turns to informal finance for funding. Every day millions of individuals and households take up a loan with a moneylender or deposit a few dollars in an informal savings club. Information asymmetry is not an issue in the informal economy, because of the proximity of the actors and their familiarity. This facilitates risk assessment and the sanctioning of deviant behaviour. Informal finance comprises "*all legal but officially unrecorded and unregulated financial activities and transactions … outside the orbit of officially regulated institutional finance.*"[2] Informal finance ranges from friends, neighbours, colleagues and other non-commercial sources, to moneylenders, landlords, traders, input or equipment suppliers and other commercial credit arrangements.[3] Informal lenders do it for profit; rotating savings and credit associations ("ROSCAs") do it for solidarity and self-help. This "informal" financial market flourishes where the formal financial market fails.[4] It is widespread.[5] Still, if moneylenders, savings clubs and other informal lenders are there to cater to the needs of the unbanked majority, what is the space for microfinance?

After all, the rapidity and convenience of moneylenders, informal savings and credit clubs or other informal mechanisms is hard to beat. The client does not need to leave the familiar neighbourhood. The moneylender lives around the corner and is available 24/7. Money is handed out on the spot. The transaction is simple, straightforward, paperless and it is all a matter of personal reputation.

BOX 2.1 Motorcycle bankers operate in large markets in West Africa. A study by D. Gentil et al. interviewed 29 motor cycle bankers in Togo and 63 in Benin.[6] Every day, they collect a fixed amount of cash against receipt from market women who do not have the time to deposit liquidities in a bank or who fear theft. He comes by every day at about the same time. The deposit amount is always the same. At the end of the day the motorcycle banker deposits the collected sum of money in a bank. The entire transaction is meant for safe keeping, no interest is earned, to the contrary a market woman has to pay a commission of 1/30 per month. The only trace of the transaction is a stamp on the monthly card confirming the payment.

> BOX 2.2 In a *"tontine,"* women with similar interests and social ties get together to finance social events of tontine members. Tontines are characterised by a very low degree of formalisation, and extensive voluntary work. The contributions vary between FCFA 10,000 and 2,000 a month ($30 and 6). Tontines can have 10, and as many as 340 members. The purpose is to put aside a small amount of money for an emergency or a social event, and to secure the support and solidarity of the group in case of need.[7]

Informal finance may be rapid, flexible and convenient, but it also has its shortcomings. Loans must be repaid within a period of a few days, at most weeks. Informal loans tend to be expensive: rates have been observed to be 2%–4% higher than bank lending rates.[8] The interest rate in West Africa ranges between 5% and 50%, with an average of 13.3% *per month*.[9] Annualised interest rate can go up to 200% and even 400%.[10] Based on 34 country reports CGAP finds that "MFI rates (are) almost always lower—usually vastly lower—than rates charged by informal lenders" (Table 2.1).[11]

Informal finance is not only expensive, it is also no guarantee against fraud either: "40% of interviewed savers in Accra had lost money through a defaulting collector."[13] There are anecdotal but recurrent stories of motorcycle bankers disappearing with the collections belonging to market women in Lomé and Cotonou.[14]

Some forms of informal finance have a particularly constraining effect: if credit transactions are tied with commodity and labour contracts, they create a double or triple bind of the borrower to the lender who may be the landlord or employer or input supplier or trader. These "interlinked contracts" can severely hamper the ability of a household-enterprise to use other options on the menu of financial instruments. In fact, it is in the interest of the lender/employer/landlord that the

Table 2.1 Interest rates compared: banks, MFIs and the informal financial sector (annual percentage rates)

2003[12]	Commercial banks (%)	MFIs (%)	Informal lenders (%)
Indonesia	18	28–63	120–720
Cambodia	18	45	120–180
Nepal	11.5–18	18–24	60–120
India	12–15	20–40	24–120
Philippines	24–29	60–80	120+
Bangladesh	10–13	20–25	180–240

12 *Microfinance: a response to market failure*

borrower/employee/tenant remains dependent and in the poverty trap.[15] In the worst case, clients bound to the moneylender in an "interlinked contract" may lose the small lot of land or other assets pledged and end up in lifelong debt bondage.[16]

In order to avoid dependency on a single creditor or deposit-taker, "household-enterprises" tend to diversify their financial transactions with several agents. The downside of such risk hedging is that they have to keep track of a host of small transactions, each with its own terms and rates. Research on financial diaries in India and Bangladesh has shown that there is a range of – mostly informal – financial instruments that an individual or a family has to keep track of. Managing this bundle of credit and debit transactions is stressful.[17] Interviews by Stuart Rutherford et al. with 250 households in India and Bangladesh showed the simultaneous use of several informal financial transactions:

Informal mutual

> Participation in a ROSCA (Rotating Savings and Loan Association)[18]
> Participation in an ASCA (Accumulating Savings and Loan Association)[19]

Informal individual

> Keeping cash at home
> Carrying cash around
> Mud bank
> Remitting money home

Informal among individuals

> Lending and borrowing interest free
> Lending and borrowing with interest
> Saving with a money guard
> Acting as a money guard
> Borrowing against pawn
> Lending against pawn
> Hire purchase of small assets
> Purchase on credit and selling on credit
> Wage advance given/taken
> Rent arrears

In the informal economy individuals can be simultaneously borrowers and lenders interacting with several people in their neighbourhood. It is not easy to keep track of how much money is owed when to whom and due when from whom. The stress can be avoided when the household-enterprise deals with a single service provider. Microfinance simplifies life, especially if you live near the poverty line. It helps to consolidate multiple financial transactions. Moreover, in contrast to informal employer-lenders or trader-lenders, microfinance institutions do not issue "interlinked" contracts, as they are in financial intermediation and not in any other business.

MFIs also allow for more flexibility than money guards in terms amounts deposited and the frequency of these deposits. There is also more discretion and privacy in the office of a MFI compared to the open-air interaction of the motorcycle banker under the eyes of nosy neighbours and other market women.

Obviously not all household-enterprises are alike in their consumer preferences. Some value convenience, return and flexibility more than costs, while other household-enterprises may have the inverse preference. At any rate, MFIs offer services that are superior at least in some respects compared to informal finance – without necessarily replacing them totally – which explains their coexistence in financial markets in the South.

Notes

1 G.A. Akerlof, The market for 'lemons': quality uncertainty and the market mechanism, *Quarterly Journal of Economics*, vol. 84, no. 3, 1970, pp. 488–500, MIT Press; M. Spence, Job market signalling, *Quarterly Journal of Economics*, vol. 87, no. 3, 1973, pp. 355–374, MIT Press; J.E. Stiglitz and A. Weiss, Andrew, Credit rationing in markets with imperfect information, *The American Economic Review*, vol. 71, no. 3, June 1981, pp. 393–410.
2 A.G. Chandavarkar, The role of Informal Credit Markets in support of Microbusinesses in developing countries, Paper presented at World Conference on Support for Microenterprises, Washington, June 1988, p. 1.
3 D. Germinidis et al., Financial systems and development: what role for the formal and informal financial sectors? OECD Development Centre 1991, p. 86.
4 E. Aryeetey, The complementary role of informal financial institutions in the retailing of credit: evaluation of innovative approaches, Regional Symposium on Savings and Credit for Development, Abidjan, April 1992; F.J.A. Bouman, *Small, Short, and Unsecured – Informal Rural Finance in India*, New Delhi, OUP, 1989; P.B. Ghate, Interaction between the formal and informal financial sectors: The Asian experience, *World Development*, vol. 20, no. 6, 1992, pp. 859–872; H.D. Seibel, Mainstreaming informal financial institutions, *Journal of Developmental Entrepreneurship*, vol. 6, no. 1, April 2001, pp. 83–95.
5 D. Germinidis, pp. 44–45, Rahman, p. 19; Chipeta, p. 149; T.A. Timberg and C.V. Aiyar, p. 43; A.G. Chandavarkar, p. 9; P.B. Ghate, passim.
6 D. Gentil (1992) et al., op. cit.; Banquiers ambulants et Opération 71 au Togo et Bénin, Working Paper 1, Social Finance Program, ILO, Geneva 1992. See also Michel Lelart, Bibliographie sur l'Epargne et le Crédit

14 *Microfinance: a response to market failure*

informels, Notes de Recherche No. 90/11 UREF/AUPELF, 1990; M. Lelart., Les Tontines et le Financement de l'Entreprise Informelle, Notes de Recherche 18, UREF-AUPELF, 1991.

7 F.J.A. Bouman, Indigenous Savings and Credit Societies in the Third World: a Message? *Savings and Development*, no. 4 (1977), pp. 181–218. Also: F.J.A. Bouman, ROSCA and ASCRA – Beyond the Financial Landscape, Conference paper presented in Wageningen (November 1992).

8 T.A. Timberg and C.V. Aiyar (1984), p. 54.

9 E. Aryeetey and F. Gockel, Mobilizing domestic resources for Capital Formation in Ghana – the role of informal financial sectors. AERC Research Papers 3, Nairobi, August 1991, p.27

10 C. Chipeta and M.L.C. Mkandawire, Links between the informal and formal/semiformal financial sectors in Malawi, AERC Research Paper, Nairobi, November 1992, p. 135 and A.G. Chandavarkar, The role of informal Credit Markets in support of Microbusinesses in developing countries, CSM Paper submitted to World Conference on Support for Microenterprises, Washington, 1988, table 9.

11 CGAP, The New Moneylenders: Are the Poor Being Exploited by High Microcredit Interest Rates?, Occasional Paper15, February 2009, p. 20.

12 CGAP, Interest rate Ceilings and Microfinance – the Story so far, Occasional Paper 9, September 2004, p. 4.

13 E. Aryeetey and F. Gockel, op. cit., p. 22.

14 D. Gentil et al., Banquiers ambulants et Opérations 71 au Togo et au Bénin, Social Finance Program, ILO, WP. 1, 1997.

15 F.J.A. Bouman and O. Hospes, *Financial Landscapes Reconstructed – The Fine art of Mapping Development*, Westview Press, 1984, pp. 179–271; Rahman and Wahid, pp. 303–321.

16 P. Bardhan, Research on Poverty and Development – 20 Years after "Redistribution with Growth", World Bank Annual Conference 1995, pp. 59–82; L. Caplan, Multiplication of social ties – The strategy of credit transactions in East Nepal, *Economic Development and Cultural Change*, vol. 20, no. 4, July 1972, pp. 691–702; P. Bose, Formal-informal sector interaction in rural credit markets, *Journal of Development Economics*, vol. 56, 1998, pp. 265–280.

17 S. Rutherford, *The Poor and Their Money*, DFID, OUP, 1999 www.jointokyo. org/mfdl/readings/PoorMoney.pdf.

 D. Collins, J. Morduch, S. Rutherford, O. Ruthven, *Portfolios of the Poor: How the World's Poor Live on $2 a Day*, Princeton UP, 2009.

18 "An instalment system for deposits and loans designed to pool small savings. Generally the holder of the first position in a sequence ROSCA ... is a pure borrower and the last a pure saver." (A.G. Chandavarkar, op. cit., p. 4). On average a ROSCA has between 15 and 40 members (H.D. Seibel, op. cit., 7).

19 In contrast to ROSCAs a residual amount of capital remains in the association. It is managed by a member and distributed at the end of an agreed period.

3 The demand for microfinance

To many it comes as a surprise to hear that the poor in low-income countries save or borrow.[1] However, we have seen that the poor constantly engage in a host of different small-scale financial transactions – informally. So, there would be a demand for microfinance provided that its services are superior to what the poor get from moneylenders, savings clubs and ROSCAs. The multitude of financial instruments in the informal economy reflects a multitude of day-to-day situations. A MFI that effectively meets this demand has to be flexible and offer products and services that respond to life cycle events, emergencies and the occasional income-generating opportunity.[2] Equity Bank in Kenya, for example, offers

> a diverse range of financial services to the low-income market that does not otherwise have access to financial services from commercial banks...: ...lump sums of money to send their children to school, to buy medicines, to respond to other shocks and emergencies that beset their households, for social and religious festivals, to save up for old age etc. – and not just ...the mono-product, working capital loan.[3]

If MFIs do not provide the required flexibility, then the poor will simply stay away or drop out: according to G. Wright "product design is one of the most important factors affecting participation." Another study[4] by Alamghir (1997) found that about 25% of non-participants did not join a microfinance institution because they were unable to make weekly savings instalments, about 15% could not make weekly loan instalments, 7% were not interested in getting a loan, and another 7% did not want to attend weekly meetings.[5]

Dropouts are not a marginal phenomenon. In Bangladesh they are in the range of 15% to 20% of all clients per year.[6] Dropouts signal dissatisfaction of clients with what the MFI has to offer, and here again it

16 *The demand for microfinance*

appears to be a lack of flexibility in product design that turns participants off: ceilings on loan amounts, unsuitable repayment schedules, obligatory group meetings, obligatory joint liability, etc. Initially MFIs focused on a particular product: working capital loans for microentrepreneurs. These were simple to manage and could be standardised. As it turned out most household-enterprises are not exactly entrepreneurially disposed that they would need working capital loans all the time, particularly if they live on $2 a day. For other poor people, certain features in the loan design just did not make sense. And most poor people do not want loans as often as the MFIs would like them to.[7]

The demand for finance is a function of the living situation. An analysis of data in the World Bank's "LSMS" (Living Standard Measurement Survey) in 13 countries shows[8] that the "extremely poor," i.e. those living on less than $1 a day, have many children and that food represents between 56% and 78% of rural household budgets and 56% and 74% of urban household budgets. The poor also spend a disproportionately large amount of money on festivities and social events. They would like to be able to save more, but cannot, and this causes them stress, day in, day out. As a result, the poor run multiple small-scale income-generating activities at the same time, without specializing in any. The poor have a sound sense of risks and quite rationally refrain from taking them.

Demand for finance varies with the level of poverty. The "extremely poor" have different needs than other segments of the poor.[9] The "extremely poor" are again different from the destitute or "ultra-poor" (widows, orphans, the chronically sick and the mobile landless).[10] Those who live on less than $2 a day are only slightly better off in terms of human resources, the quality of their dwelling, food security and vulnerability and assets.[11] The poor are not homogeneous with regard to their demand for finance. The intensity and diversity of their involvement in small scale financial transactions varies with the level of poverty. The "Graduation Program"[12] by CGAP and the Ford Foundation shows that it is possible to reach out even to the "ultra-poor," with food aid, savings promotion, skills training and asset transfers to jump-start an income generating activity, from which point they can start to interact with a MFI. So there seems to be a limit in the depth of outreach. "Microfinance providers in Uganda reach low-income households in both rural and urban areas, but not the poorest of the poor. Those significantly below the poverty line do not seem to join Ugandan MFIs."[13]

Who, then, are the poor who use the services of MFIs, for more or less long periods? Obviously, there are variations from country to country but a recurrent feature is that these clients are self-employed, they work at and from home, and employ family members occasionally: a

The demand for microfinance   17

street corner shop, street vendors, simple trades and crafts, small tenant farmers and service providers.

> The majority of household-enterprises are in the trading sector, ... transformation of agricultural goods, artisanal activities such as making custom furniture; construction; and services such as food service (making and selling snacks or lunches), tailoring, transport, and personal services (barbering and hairdressing).[14]

Broadly speaking, these clients are near the poverty line, some below, some seasonally below and above, and some just above. Not whether one is poor, but how poor one is determines the conditions for demand for microfinance, whether loans, deposits, insurance, payments and any other financial service.

Typical microfinance institutions have loan portfolios with clients that can be described as "household-enterprises"[15], i.e. own-account (self-employed) enterprises that employ family members without paying them. Household-enterprises have financial profiles of both consuming and producing entities. Banks which makes them impossible to deal with for banks which are used to differentiate. For the financial institution it is then harder to assess the risks of loan default. There are distinct credit rating algorithms for consumer lending and for SME finance that allow a fairly precise idea of the probability of default. Not so with household-enterprises where, the financing needs for consumption and investment are intertwined.

From the financing perspective this raises a number of issues:

- The capitalisation of household-enterprises is comparatively low because they are not specialised.
- The activities they engage in require low thresholds of start-up capital, like services, trade, processing – not manufacturing.
- Because of the low initial capital requirements, household-enterprises are faced with competition by individuals operating in the same line of business.

> BOX 3.1 Anyone strolling over a traditional African open-air market is struck by the long rows of stalls displaying the same kind of textiles, the same kind of household utensils, the same kind of just about any consumer item. There is little price differentiation. Proximity and mutual observation make sure that vendors stick to the trade line on pricing.

18   *The demand for microfinance*

- Because of the low returns generated by a household-enterprise, the family needs to diversify into other income generating activities in order to survive.

> BOX 3.2 A typical microfinance client of a MFI in India is involved in many economic activities. In a given year, she works for herself (self-employment) for about 20% of the time, e.g. in rearing cattle or working on her own agricultural field or doing some small manufacturing. For the rest of the employment duration, she works for others, for instance, as wage labour on the fields of larger farmers or at public works sites. Besides these, she may also take up community work for which she may or may not get remuneration.[16]

- As household-enterprises operate with low profit margins, any returns – if they materialise – are not reinvested in the same or another income-generating activity, but are used to bolster household consumption or set aside to protect the family against unforeseeable but certain catastrophic events.

  The effective absorption capacity of financial services by household-enterprises, is difficult to read, certainly for banks and even for MFIs. Information asymmetry, moral hazard and adverse selection characterise the financing environment of household-enterprises. A case in point is the price elasticity of demand. MFIs assume that client demand is fairly inelastic for emergency loans or loans for unexpected life cycle events. This is plausible. But when it comes to loan products for income generation, it is not at all clear how client demand reacts to changes in the interest rate, because some income generating opportunity may arise in an unexpected situation (less elastic) or in a recurrent activity (more elastic).

- Household-enterprises are more risk-averse than specialised microenterprises. The term "household-enterprise" emphasises location and labour use, in contrast to the term "microenterprises," which puts the emphasis on the scale of operations. This is plausible as the family's welfare would be directly impaired by investments that yield returns only in the distant future. Being in a constant survival mode, household-enterprises plan for weeks ahead, at best for a few months. They cannot afford to commit important amounts of cash to outlays the outcome of which is uncertain. Because of risk aversion, the activity

The demand for microfinance   19

funded is likely to be barely profitable, which is not exactly what MFIs expect.

- The fungibility of money makes is difficult to track the flow of funds within a household-enterprise. A three months loan of $500 that had initially been foreseen to purchase building materials for an extension of the street corner shop may be diverted to pay for the transport of a family member to the nearest dispensary and medical expenses. The initially intended use of the loan would have strengthened the earning capacity of the household-enterprise – not so the actual use of the loan. The creditor is confronted with a client whose repayment capacity is impaired.
- Being anchored in a family and drawing heavily on family labour household-enterprises are more affected by life cycle events (birth, marriage, death). In informal economies life cycle events entail disproportionate expenditures.

> BOX 3.3 In South African townships, for example, people have been observed to spend between R2,350.00 ($391.67) up to R15,000.00 ($2,500.00), i.e. 5–36 times the average monthly household income of R412.73 ($68.78).[17]

Lenders may thus be confronted with substantial loan demands for social consumption affecting the repayment capacity often for years. Life cycle events are to some extent foreseeable, but this is not the case with accidents and illnesses affecting members of the family in a household-enterprise. In the absence of a clear separation between family budget and enterprise budget, life cycle events influence the net debt position and diminish the debt absorption capacity for any income generating activity.

Household-enterprises represent the bulk in the loan portfolios of most MFIs., but there are other categories of clients. Al Majmoua, a MFI in Lebanon for example, finances

employees not registered in the National Social Security Fund (NSSF) or those whose salary is not sufficient to receive a bank loan..., low income individuals wanting to fix or improve their houses..., spouses of existing clients with good repayment history, to pay for the schooling expenses of their children....[18]

20 *The demand for microfinance*

What emerges is a demand for microfinance products and services that are preferable to clients compared to informal finance, and at the same time without the nuisances of banking: microfinance needs to be prompt, affordable, flexible and innovative – and not ask too many questions.

Notes

1 See S. Rutherford, *The Economics of Poverty: How Poor People Manage Their Money*. Washington, Corporation for Enterprise Development, 2002; S. Rutherford, *The Poor and Their Money*. Oxford India Paperbacks, 2001; D. Collins, J. Morduch, S. Rutherford and O. Ruthven, *Portfolios of the Poor – How the World's Poor Live on $2 a Day*, Princeton UP 2009.
2 G. Wright, Understanding and Assessing the demand for microfinance, Microsave, Paris, June 2005.
3 G. Wright, op. cit., p. 5.
4 D.A.H. Alamgir, Review of current interventions for hardcore poor in Bangladesh and how to reach them with financial services, Paper presented at the Credit Development Forum Workshop on Dropout Features, Extending Outreach and How to Reach the Hard-core Poor, BIDS, Dhaka, 1997.
5 G. Wright, *Microfinance Systems: Designing Quality Financial Services for the Poor*. Dhaka, The University Press Limited, 2000.
6 R. L. Meyer, The Demand for flexible Microfinance Products: lessons from Bangladesh, *Journal of International Development*, vol. 14, no. 3, April 2002.
7 CGAP, Are We Overestimating Demand for Microloans? Brief April 2008.
8 Banerjee, Abhijit, V. and Esther Duflo. 2007. The economic lives of the poor. *Journal of Economic Perspectives*, vol. 21, no. 1, pp. 141–168.
9 This explains the interest of MFIs and their donors to find out how poor clients actually are; see for example CGAP, Poverty Assessment Tool, 2003 intended for implementation by MFIs. Another tool is the Progress out of Poverty Index. This has to be seen in a context when it was expected of MFIs to demonstrate that they were reaching out to the "poorest of the poor."
10 G.Wright, op.cit., 2000, p. 3
11 CGAP, Poverty Assessment Tool, op.cit., p. 8
12 CGAP, Reaching the Poorest – Lessons from the Graduation Model, Focus Note 69, March 2011.
13 A. Carlton, H. Manndorff, A. Obara, W. Reiter, E. Rhyne, Microfinance in Uganda, Austrian Ministry of Foreign Affairs, Department for Development Cooperation, Vienna December 2001, pp. 19–20
14 L. Fox and T. Sohnesen, Household Enterprises in Sub-Saharan Africa – Why They Matter for Growth, Jobs, and Livelihoods, Policy Research Working Paper 6184, World Bank, August 2012, p. 13
15 This definition leaves out the agricultural sector, as the employment of family members on the farm is more widespread than in other sectors, and not specific to low income economies.
16 GIAN Survey for Microfinance and Public Policy, ILO/Palgrave 2007.
17 J.Roth, Informal Micro-Finance Schemes: the case of funeral insurance in South Africa, Social Finance Programme, Working Paper 22, ILO, 2000, p. 12.
18 www.almajmoua.org/FinancialServices.aspx

4 Products and services

Microfinance products are have grown in diversity in response to diverse needs in very different markets by very heterogeneous client groups. Increasingly, these products have grown in diversity in response are designed so as to help achieve to one or more of the "Sustainable Development Goals (SDGs)."[1] In other words, beyond financial inclusion microfinance products are expected to hold the key to goods, services, facilities and infrastructure that the world community considers vital.

A case in point are micro housing loans, which contribute to SDG 11 (sustainable cities and communities). MHFC, a MFI in India, has specialised in micro mortgage loans that help poor households acquire their own apartment or house. It is not the only MFI with this focus. There is already a critical mass of similar MFIs out there that prompted Triple Jump, a social investment manager to create Microbuild Fund, which refinances 33 MFIs that offer microfinance for housing. Microfinance can also ease access to schooling and education. Kashf, a MFI in Pakistan, provides loans for private school owners to improve access to primary education in rural areas. There is a lively market in renewable energy loans.[2] Food security, another Sustainable Development Goal, is increasingly being addressed in agricultural micro-insurance schemes. Women's World Banking's maternal health programme ("*Caregiver Hospital Cash Policy*") promotes hybrid insurance and savings products to members of its affiliates in Jordan (MFW), Uganda (Finance Trust), Morocco (Al Amana) and Peru (Ariquipa). In short: there is more to microfinance products than the usual working capital loan.

A closer look at the list of products reveals the conspicuous absence of an otherwise standard retail service in banking: **consumer loans**. For many years, the accepted consensus was that microfinance

22 *Products and services*

institutions should *not* offer consumer loans, because they do not generate a surplus revenue out of which the loan can be paid back. For people living near the poverty line consumer loans are a slippery slope to over-indebtedness. In actual fact, though, MFIs may have been inadvertently providing consumer loans, whenever a credit intended for income generation was diverted by the client to some other purpose, to cover unforeseen expenses related to accidents, illnesses, festivities or life cycle events. Preferable would, of course, be savings to avoid going into debt in the first place, but that is not always available. Without explicitly discarding consumer lending, most MFIs – or rather those that subscribe to the Smart Campaign's Client Protection Principles – commit to prevent over-indebtedness and "take adequate care in all phases of the credit process to determine that clients have the capacity to repay without becoming over-indebted."[3]

MFIs differ in the range of products offered, as the following examples illustrate:

Sathapana, a microfinance bank in Cambodia, offers several savings schemes: sight, term and other deposit services; it also provides revolving credit, overdraft facilities, term loans, housing loans and remittance services within Cambodia and abroad. It is equipped to finance trade operations and provide payroll services.

SEWA Bank, a microfinance institution organised as a cooperative for self-employed poor women in India, offers five different savings schemes suited to different savings needs of its members: a daily savings scheme, a "worry riddance" scheme, a special occasion scheme, a housing fund scheme and a buying gold scheme. Loan products are for housing, house and workshop improvement and the special needs of wives of laid-off workers in a nearby mill. The design of these products reflects the three main drivers of the demand for finance in the informal economy: life cycle events, emergency and opportunity.

Al Majmoua, an NGO-type MFI in Lebanon affiliated to the Save the Children network, offers loans to groups of 3–10 women entrepreneurs, but also loans to owners of existing microbusinesses and few cases of starts-ups; SME loans to owners of small and medium enterprises, and ICT loans to owners of existing or start-up businesses in information and communication technology located in rural areas. In addition Al Majmoua designed specific products for the young ("Yalla Shabab Loan"), Worker Loans (for employees not registered in the National Social Security Fund (NSSF) or those whose salary is not sufficient to receive a bank loan) and home improvement loans to low-income individuals. "Back to School loans" are targeted at spouses of existing clients with good repayment history, to pay for the schooling expenses of their children. "Damej loans" are available for individuals with special needs with existing or start-up businesses.

Three MFIs with a wide range of financial products. That reflect differences in demand – or what the MFI perceives as demand. On the one end, there is a succinct range of deposit and loan products that is hardly distinguishable from a bank's (Sathapana) and at the other end there is a multitude of loan schemes tailored to the needs of very specific client groups (Al Majmoua). Other factors that determine what the range, conditions and volume of financial and non-financial products and services are resources, delivery costs and technology.

Different MFIs finance themselves differently. Some call more on grants for equity, others rely heavily on credit lines (subsidised or on market terms), or on client deposits. The **pattern of refinancing** itself depends on the legal form of a MFI, which matters to the capacity to take deposits. NGOs and most NBFIs (non-bank financial intermediaries) do not offer deposit products because they do not have the authorisation to do so.[4] MFIs that are organised as cooperatives can take deposits – but only from their members, generally not from the general public. By contrast banks can take deposits as they are under the supervision of the central bank. Table 4.1 compares the patterns of refinancing of three MFIs with distinct legal forms.

All three MFIs – regardless of legal form – are substantially subsidised with start-up grants. All three dispose of a comfortable debt/equity ratio, far better than what would be required of commercial banks. All three resort to soft loans, i.e. credit lines that are made available by DFIs and social investors at below market rates. Where

Table 4.1 The legal form largely determines the liabilities structure

USD	Cooperative MFI	NBFI MFI	NGO MFI
Equity on a grant basis	6,438,799	1,582,531	1,435,192
	1,890,997	585,635	984,840
Deposits	14,723,415	0	0
Commercial loans	0	100,000	0
Soft loans, short-term	504,434	4,297,354	1,070,258
Soft loans, long-term	517,313	0	0
Total liabilities	22,183,961	5,979,885	2,505,450

24 *Products and services*

they differ is the capacity to raise deposits (only cooperatives can do that) and the use of commercial loans (only the NBFI).

The capacity to take deposits and thus the ability to offer a range of deposit products matters not just to the MFI – but also to clients. Clients want to have a facility to set aside small amounts of cash safely. MFIs have more control over deposits than over other types of resources: they can adjust the rate of remuneration, or the minimum amount to be deposited, or the conditions for cash withdrawal, etc. They would not have this flexibility with a credit line that requires negotiations with a creditor. Savings-based MFIs are also more likely to be better managed. Clients have a stake in the institution and tend to scrutinise decisions by management more rigorously. More and more, NGO-type MFIs are therefore changing their legal form to be able to collect deposits.

The second main determinant of products on offer is the **costs** involved in developing, distributing and managing a product. Generally, microfinance faces high transaction costs, higher than in banks, because of the small transaction amounts involved, the short contractual cycles and the remoteness of clients. Operating expenses make up over 50% of the average yield in microfinance, far ahead of financing expenses (i.e. the costs of credit lines, etc.) some 25% with the remaining 25% for loan losses and profit.[5]

Regulatory constraints, also influence the range of products. They can force a MFI to stop offering loans that could be provided only at interest rates exceeding the ceiling imposed by public authorities. In West Africa, for example, the UEMOA (West Africa Economic and Monetary Union) set in 2013 an interest rate ceiling for MFIs at 24% annualised.[6] Considering that the average yield of MFIs in Africa was 25% in 2011[7] one can imagine that MFIs are bound to calculate thoroughly before introducing products and services for which they would have to charge rates that collide with central bank rules.

Some microfinance products are associated with even higher costs. A case in point is micro-insurance.[8] There is a demand for a financial product that protects a household-enterprise against unforeseeable shocks and catastrophes. But to deliver micro-insurance, MFIs need to have especially skilled staff, which may need to be recruited. Some MFIs prefer instead to offer micro-insurance in partnership with specialised insurers. Similar partnership arrangements are found in micro-leasing, payment services, e-wallets and non-financial services. Such partnerships are not for free.

Products and services 25

The third main determinant of the product range of MFIs is **technology**. Technology can lead to the design of new products, and reduce transaction costs so much so that products that otherwise would have to be phased out now become feasible for the MFI to offer. The average cost per withdrawal transaction in Mexican and Colombian banks has been halved from $0.88 to $0.43 after the banks had replaced teller services in conventional "bricks and mortar" bank branches with agent banking,[9] involving supermarkets, gas stations, mobile phone shops, etc. "In an international comparison of 26 banks, McKay and Pickens (2010) found that branchless banking (including mobile money) was 19% cheaper on average than alternative services. At low transaction amounts or for informal money transfer options, this difference more than doubled."[10] Safaricom's M-Pesa was routinely one-third to one-half as expensive as alternative payment systems. Technology enters the equation because the client and transaction details are transmitted by cell phones, debit and prepaid cards. Other applications of technology further expand the range of microfinance products: internet banking, ATMs and mobile phone-based transactions directly with the bank/MFI/MNO. M-banking to date has largely been driven by mobile network operators and some large banks.[11]

In 2016, 90% of the Kenyan adult population, 16 million Kenyans, had an account with M-Pesa. The outreach of mobile banking far exceeds that of bank branches or ATMs: for every 100,000 Kenyans there are 11 ATMs, 6 commercial bank branches but 538 mobile banking agent outlets.[12] In 2016, mobile money was available in 93 countries via 271 services, through agents or MNOs for a total of over 500 million registered accounts globally.[13] However, while mobile banking in Africa is still largely synonymous with making payments. This is slowly changing. Some MFIs are beginning to partner with mobile network operators to piggyback genuine microfinance products onto cell phone-based transactions. For example, M-Pesa is now also being used as a vehicle to commercialise micro-insurance ("Kilimo Salama"). "M-Kesho" is another example; it offers micro-savings, micro-insurance and micro-loans and was developed by Equity Bank, a microfinance bank in co-operation with Safaricom, M-Pesa's owner MNO. It is a safe guess that in the near future technology will both make classic microfinance products less costly to deliver and hence more affordable for the poor and at the same time lead to new products building on payments and G2P transfers like child allowance and pensions.

26 *Products and services*

Non-financial services

The analysis of microfinance products would not be complete with a look at non-financial services. In contrast to most banks[14] microfinance institutions also offer non-financial services. In fact, some have argued that it is precisely the integration of financial and non-financial services that is the hallmark of microfinance. Actually, it should not be surprising that MFIs offer non-financial services, labelled often "social" services. After all, this is in line with the double bottom line of MFIs. As with so many other issues in microfinance there are debates and controversies about the right way forward for MFIs. Advocates of the minimalist approach want MFIs to concentrate on credit and other financial services, whilst proponents of the integrated or "credit plus" school of thought claim that mere finance is not going to make a difference.[15]

Non-financial services target either the enterprise or the household component of the household-enterprise: business development, market information, referral services linking the client to networks and associations, skills training and financial management are typical non-financial services for income generation in a very small enterprise, while health and nutrition courses, functional literacy, social empowerment, gender sensitisation and care services and sanitation address the household side of the client. Customers appreciate both kinds of non-financial services,[16] although they often have to pay for them. There is some evidence that clients benefit from these services. A study[17] of the impact of non-financial services offered by Microfinance Banks in Nigeria on 384 women entrepreneurs showed that – while not all non-financial services made a difference – "training and network meetings ... did influence... the performance of the women entrepreneurs."

A randomised controlled trial by D. Karlan and M. Valdivia[18] in Peru found that business education (i.e. money management, budgeting, marketing and sales management) had positive effects on the performance of micro-entrepreneurs when combined with credit. Clients who receive financial services *and* business education show higher incomes compared to clients who had contracted only financial services.

For the average MFI, providing non-financial services needs to be well considered. A MFI incurs substantial costs offering non-financial services, especially if it decides to provide them itself – and not in partnership with a specialised NGO. There are also benefits for the MFI. Clients who are trained, advised and informed about market opportunities are more likely to stay in business, grow and pay back the loan in time.[19] Moreover, non-financial services are a way for a MFI to get to know a client better: how regularly does she attend group meetings?

How actively does she participate? Can she articulate her point of view and interest? How does she interact with other group members? How do they respond to her presence and participation? Observations of this kind address the information asymmetry between an otherwise opaque informal household-enterprise and the MFI. Client participation in non-financial services functions almost as a collateral substitute.

Moreover, MFIs can exert leverage on clients with overdue loans by withholding access to training programmes and other popular non-financial services. Non-financial services appear to create in customers a sense of "belonging" to a MFI. An illustration is "credit with education." MFIs affiliated to the Freedom from Hunger network combine a financial with a non-financial service, "credit with education." The care and attention transmitted in the education part appear to have reinforced customer loyalty towards "their" MFI more than a mere loan product would have done.[20]

On balance and according to a recent study of MFIs in 77 countries by R. Lensink et al.[21] "the provision of non-financial services does not harm nor improve MFIs' financial sustainability and efficiency.... (In fact) ... it is associated with improved loan quality and greater depth of outreach." This would suggest that as long as clients appreciate these services, MFIs should not refrain from developing and reinforcing them, even if they do not generate revenues. At least they do not seem to do any harm.[22]

Micro-grants – conditional and other

There is a type of service on offer by some MFIs that many would not even consider a financial service, namely grants. Financial services are based on contracts and on reciprocal obligations: a loan will be paid back to the lender and a deposit must be returned to the depositor. Grants do not have this circularity; a grantee must not give back the grant. Grants are being used in microfinance not exactly like gifts, but with strings attached. The grantee cannot do with the grant as she pleases. Grants in the context of microfinance are better labelled "conditional micro-grants." They are part of an arsenal of instruments to morally oblige the recipient to a particular use of the grant that serves as a stepping stone to eventually reach a level of incomes and stability that allows the absorption of debt and constitution of savings. It is the *future* debt absorption capacity that justifies micro-grants in the *present*.

A common scenario for the use of conditional micro-grants is a post-disaster situation, where individuals find themselves all of a sudden deprived of physical and financial assets. Another application of

28   *Products and services*

conditional micro-grants is the destitute who are too vulnerable to take on any debt and who need skills and confidence to build up slowly a productive capacity. The best-known example of a grant used as a stepping stone for future microfinance services is the "Income Generation for Vulnerable Groups Development (IGVGD) program" in Bangladesh.[23] The IGVGD is intended for rural women who have little or no income earning opportunities, hence no debt absorption capacity. A conventional microloan would only push these hardcore poor more into destitution. The grant consists of an in-kind donation of food grain. This is embedded in a progressive graduation process allowing these women to participate eventually, after a year or more, in savings and credit schemes. Of a million rural women reached through IGVGD, two-thirds have successfully graduated.

Another example is the scheme of conditional cash grants promoted by Trickle-Up, a US based NGO, which provides grants of US$50 to $100 via local community organisations to stabilise household consumption, "in the event of a failed crop, sudden illness, or other setback."[24] Recipients of this grant have to follow coaching and training sessions and accept visits at home. The process is geared towards an eventual income generating capacity.[25] The main conditionality lies in the obligation to use the grant for a particular activity – and not for anything else. To ensure compliance recipients must also join groups of five or more people. "Three months after the first instalment of US$50, and if the group has met the required conditions, it receives the second US$50, again as a grant with conditions attached."[26]

Clearly, what microfinance institutions have on offer is very different from products and services that one would encounter in retail banking. The range and nature of these products reflect the fact that MFIs have a double bottom line and seek to remain responsive – some more, some less – to the needs of clients even if a business case cannot be made in the short term in every single case. The hybrid nature of MFIs as social enterprises shows also in the way these products and services are delivered to clients, which is the subject of the next chapter.

Notes

1 Adopted in September 2015 by the UN General Assembly these new goals apply globally and commit countries to end by 2030 all "forms of poverty, fight inequalities and tackle climate change, while ensuring that no one is left behind" (www.un.org/sustainabledevelopment/development-agenda).
2 The European Microfinance Platform has an action group on Green Microfinance. The Platform supported the preparation of the "Green Index 2.0," a tool to assess environmental performance in the Microfinance

sector. Jointly with the MIX, the EMFP published in 2015 "Assessing Green Microfinance: Qualitative and Quantitative Indicators for Measuring Environmental Performance." There are now mobile phone-based service providers of solar energy: MPOKA in Kenya; MOBISOL, MGP, SOLAR NOW, Bboxx.

3 www.smartcampaign.org/about/smart-microfinance-and-the-client-protection-principles.

4 With some exceptions: in Cambodia NBFIs are supervised by the central bank and are allowed to take deposits.

5 R. Rosenberg, S. Gaul, W. Ford, and O. Tomilova, Microcredit Interest Rates and Their Determinants, CGAP, Access to Finance Forum, Reports by CGAP and its Partners No. 7, June 2013, p. 21.

6 www.cgap.org/blog/worrying-trend-interest-rate-caps-africa.

7 Ibid.

8 Seen from the microfinance perspective, micro-insurance is just one financial service of several in the wide portfolio of services; seen from the micro-insurance angle, microfinance institutions are just one of several distribution channels (C. Churchill, Insurance for the poor: definitions and innovations, *Handbook of Microfinance*, op. cit., p. 547).

9 CGAP, Slide 11, presentation "Branchless Banking 101," by Sarah Rotman, March 29, 2012.

10 K. Donovan. *Mobile Money for Financial Inclusion, Information and Communications for Development*, World Bank, 2012, p. 63.

11 "MFIs have by and large not played a significant role in the implementation of m-banking services" CGAP, Branchless Banking op. cit., p. 1.

12 GSMA, State of the Industry Report on Mobile Money, Decade Edition: 2006–2016, 2017, p. 15.

13 GSMA, 2015 – State of the Industry Report Mobile Money, p. 9 and GSMA, State of the Industry Report on Mobile Money, Decade Edition: 2006–2016, 2017, p. 2.

14 In fact, some banks do provide non-financial services, however to a different target market, namely SMEs: IFC, Why Banks in Emerging Markets Are Increasingly Providing Non-financial Services to Small and Medium Enterprises, Washington, DC, 2012.

15 J. Ledgerwood, Microfinance Handbook – an institutional and financial perspective, World Bank, Sustainable Banking with the Poor, 1999, p. 65.

16 A study by O. Biosca et al. (Microfinance Non-Financial Services: A Key for Poverty Alleviation? Lessons from Mexico, October 2011, U Sheffield, Sheffield Economic Research Paper Series, SERP Number: 2011021) finds that business development services and preventive health services "reduce the clients' likelihood of being under the asset poverty line."

17 A.Ch. Dikki et al., Impact of non-financial services of Microfinance Banks (MFBs) on the performance of women entrepreneurs in Nigeria, *European Journal of Business and Management*, vol. 6, no. 34, 2014.

18 D. Karlan and M. Valdivia (2009), Teaching entrepreneurship: impact of business training on microfinance clients and institutions, *The Review of Economics and Statistics*, vol. 93, no. 2, May 2011, pp. 510–527.

19 CGAP, Microfinance, Grants and Non-financial Responses to Poverty Reduction: Where Does Microcredit Fit In?, Focus Note 20, December 2002, p. 10.

30 *Products and services*

20 B. Gray, M. Gash, S. Reeves, B. Crookston, Microfinance – a sustainable platform for non-financial services. *Progress in Economics Research*, vol. 20, 2011, pp. 163–182.
21 R. Lensink, R. Mersland, N.T. Hong Vu and S. Zamore, Do microfinance institutions benefit from integrating financial and nonfinancial services?, *Applied Economics*, 2017, DOI:10.1080/00036846.2017.1397852.
22 Lensink et al., op. cit., p. 14.
23 S. Hashemi et al., Linking Microfinance and Safety Programs to include the poorest, CGAP Focus Note 21 May 2001.
24 https://trickleup.org/graduation-approach/.
25 Ibid.
26 Shivani Puri and Peter van Rooij, Microfinance and Poverty – A Comparative Assessment of the Impact of Conditional Micro-grants and Micro-credit in Nepal and Uganda, ILO, Social Finance Program, ILO, Geneva unpublished working paper, p. 10.

5 Methods and techniques

Microfinance institutions have different goals than banks. The products and services offered by MFIs are also quite different from what banks offer. Microfinance products are also different in the way they are delivered. In this chapter we will look at the main methods and techniques of doing microfinance practically: selecting clients on the basis of their poverty status ("targeting"), organising clients into groups ("joint liability groups"), securing loans with instruments that have little or no market value ("collateral substitution") and combining financial and non-financial services. Each technique reflects an effort to reconcile the needs of poor clients with the institutional interest to ensure profitability. Every one of them stands for the double bottom line in microfinance.

Targeting

Targeting is the selection of a beneficiary group to ensure its eligibility. Usually associated with welfare programmes, incomes policies or the distribution of subsidies, grants and allocations[1] targeting is also a characteristic practice in microfinance. Microfinance institutions select their clients in line with their mission and their double bottom line. MFIs in general reach out to those whom commercial service providers find too remote, opaque or small to cater to. MFIs, in addition, specify the sort of poor that suits their mission.

Individual characteristics are the most obvious criteria: for example, women in general, or – more specifically – illiterate women heads of households, or – even more exclusively – illiterate women heads of household in rural areas. Targeting on the basis of income generating activities informs about the client's debt absorption capacity. Targeting can be based on place of residence of clients, which has implications for the MFI's operational costs in financial service delivery. The degree of formalisation is another criterion used in targeting. A client

32 *Methods and techniques*

whose activity is registered by the municipality and who pays taxes and social security contributions, whose activity is recorded in financial statements, is obviously more transparent, easier to appraise and less of a risk than completely informal clients. All of these and many more eligibility criteria can be defined more or less restrictively. In real life targeting criteria tend to overlap (Table 5.1).

> ASA, a MFI in India, targets « *rural women below the poverty line in drought affected areas where Dalits form the majority of the population* ». CVECA, a MFI in Burkina Faso, has a wider definition of its target market, it determines simply who is *not* eligible: « *not the young, no wage earners* ». Targeting can be pushed to an extreme so much so that a full-fledged household income and asset survey would be required to identify clients, as in the case of TYM in Vietnam, which defines its target group as « *women in poor households earning less than $ 6.5 a month and total assets of no more than $ 1000; between 18 and 55 years, good physical condition*».

Of course, MFIs do not always live up to their mission declarations. Ambitious statements released at the launch of a MFI can get diluted or ignored over time as the client portfolio expands. There are no immediate

Table 5.1 Poverty targeting strategies by selected African MFIs[1]

MFIs	Targets	Focus on women	Geographical focus	Product design attractive to poor
CREDO, Burkina	Poor women	x	x	x
CRS, Senegal	Very poor, especially women	x	x	x
DECSI, Ethiopia	Very poor, motivated by YGA	x	x	x
DID, Mali	Disadvantaged	x	x	x
FFH, Ghana	Poor families	x	x	x
KWFT, Kenya	Low income, economically active women	x		x
SEF, S. Africa	Very poor micro-entrepreneurs		x	

[1] Coady International Institute, How Microfinance Providers Target the Poor – a compendium of strategies, 1999, p. xvi.

Methods and techniques 33

consequences if a MFI strays from its declared target market. The only nuisance is that after a while owners, stakeholders, donors and other supporters begin to ask critical questions about the MFI's strategy.

Targeting techniques range from identifying and actively going towards the client to a more indirect and hands-off approach, which leaves it to the discretion of the client to make the first step. Targeting can mean measures to discourage and exclude the non-poor.[2] When defining its targeting strategy, a MFI can rely on available tested scorecards for the measurement of poverty: the "Progress out of Poverty Index (PPI)" and the "Poverty Assessment Tool (PAT)."[3]

The downside of targeting for the MFI is that it limits risk diversification. From a financial angle targeting can thus lead to suboptimal returns. Obviously in some markets there is little diversification of the loan portfolio possible. If 70% of all rural women in a defined area are engaged in poultry raising, then the MFI's decision to select and target poultry raising as the income generating activity makes sense: there are few other income generating activities that it could diversify into – at least, not in the short term.

Despite limited diversification opportunities, targeting very poor clients does not seem to be detrimental for the MFI's returns, as Table 5.2[4] shows. It compares the average total expense ratio and the gross portfolio yield of three types of MFIs: those that target the very poor ("low end"), other MFIs that target not so poor people ("high end") and a third group with a clientele of mixed poverty levels. The net portfolio yield appears to be highest in MFIs that target the very poor.

It has been argued that targeting leads to new discriminations, as groups are excluded that fall in the crack between mainstream banking and microfinance. It can also lead to a misallocation of scarce resources if newly emerging activities are ignored because targeting is

Table 5.2 Targeting and the implications for expenses and yields

Source: MBB 2006 (2004 data) %	*Target low end*	*Target broad*	*Target high*
Total expense ratio	25.4	22.2	16.8
Real gross pf yield	31.2	27.2	22.2
Real net yield	5.8	5.0	5.4

Explanations: Target market "low end": average balance per borrower/GNI per head < 20% and < $ 150%; Target market "broad": average balance per borrower/GNI per head > 20% and < 150%; Target market "high end": average balance per borrower/GNI per head > 150% and < 275%; Total expense ratio: adjusted (financial + net loan loss + operating) expenses/average total assets (%); Real gross portfolio yield: adjusted yield on gross portfolio (nominal) − (inflation rate)/(1 + inflation rate).

34   *Methods and techniques*

too slow to adapt to new market trends. Changes in the distribution of incomes and assets in a local market may not be duly reflected in an MFI's targeting; it may become obsolete unless constantly updated. Another common criticism is that for targeting to be really precise and relevant MFIs would need to incur substantial costs so much so that it is no longer cost effective,[5] not to mention the social costs.[6] Still, despite these reservations, MFIs are likely to continue to single out whom they want to support and promote – a natural inclination for an entity with a double bottom line.

Groups or individuals?

Mainstream banks expect a prospective borrower to pledge a piece of land, a building, equipment or other moveable assets as security. Microfinance institutions ready to deal with a market segment of informal clients often cannot do that, because their clients do not have assets with a stable commercial value and identifiable property rights. Still MFIs need to protect themselves against loan default. In order to overcome this problem, microfinance institutions organise clients into groups bound by joint liability, where all group members are treated as being in default if one group member does not repay. The social pressure within the group serves as a substitute for formal enforcement mechanisms used in conventional banking: "group lending provides a way for credit markets to harness such non-market institutions to enforce loan repayment."[7]

MFIs organise clients or invite them to constitute groups, usually between 5 and 12 individuals. This arrangement has several advantages for the MFI: the group is liable for repayment, and thus the MFIs can contain the risk of loan default. The MFI also externalises screening and enforcement costs to the joint liability groups. Moreover, the MFI does not need to bother about the appraisal of minuscule loan applications or have staff run after clients to collect instalments due. Group lending therefore has advantages for the MFI associated with economies of scale.[8] Another attractive feature of groups is that they make it easier to organise training, sensitisation and other non-financial services. Observation of the behaviour and interaction of individuals in groups gives the MFI insights about client disposition to risk and obligations.[9] Above all: it allows them to reach out to the very poor who have no assets whatsoever.

Obviously, group formation stands and falls with the cohesion of the group. In individualistic cultures people hesitate to join a group, and if they are prodded into joining, they may leave as soon as their individual credit demand is met. Even in more community-oriented cultures,

Table 5.3 Group versus individual lending: cost implications

MBB No.12 2006 (2004 data) %	Individual lending	Mixed	Group lending
Operating expenses	12.4	15.4	33.1
Loan loss provisions	1.4	0.7	1.7
Financial expenses	5.7	4.4	5.4
Profitability (FSS)	124	115	96

it is common that groups fall apart if individual group members evolve on different economic paths and display heterogeneous financial needs. The dropout rate in joint liability groups has been observed to be as high as 38% in groups in Colombia.[10] There have also been instances where entire groups conspire against the MFI to wilfully default. Clearly, group lending with joint liability is not a guarantee for correct repayment performance.

Does it work? The record is mixed: group lending does not seem to "yield higher rates of loan repayment than conventional lending programs."[11] What matters is whether or not the group retains a certain "punishment capability,"[12] and that in turn depends on the size of the group: groups with more than 30 members are likely to be less cohesive. The homogeneity amongst members also matters: women-only groups for example seem to do better than mixed groups. Microloans should be for ongoing income generating activities, not for start-ups. There should be a good mix between income generating activities, yet not too much so as to allow the group to make an informed judgement on the risks and returns of a loan project proposed by a group member. Possibly the most important determinant for group cohesion is that the group itself selects its members – and not the MFI.[13]

Table 5.3 compares the efficiency of MFIs using different delivery techniques: individual, mixed and solidarity lending. Overall individual lending means lower operating expenses for the MFI. The externalisation of transaction costs in group lending seems to be outweighed by other cost effects, including measures to keep groups together.

Other collateral substitutes

Collateral is useful, provided the ownership status on assets can be quickly verified in the appropriate up-to-date registries. Collateral is also useful if the asset taken as collateral can be easily liquidated out of court in direct negotiations between lender and borrower. To be meaningful to the borrower, collateral should leave productive assets like essential tools and equipment in the borrower's possession so as

36 *Methods and techniques*

to preserve her capacity to generate income. Most of these conditions do not hold in low-income countries with high levels of financial exclusion. The legal and administrative infrastructure is simply not there for conventional collateralisation. In response, microfinance institutions found ways around the lack of collateral, by improvising with instruments that make the borrower respect repayment obligations, without lawyers and courts. These substitutes make up for the lack of tangible, liquid assets to secure the lender against an eventual loan default.

Joint liability is such a collateral substitute, in fact the best known. Other substitutes occasionally used are jewellery and other personal valuables, driving licences and other documents, household goods and family items of a high sentimental value. These fictitious "assets" have little cash value, too insignificant to justify the costs involved in the process of repossession and liquidation. The usefulness of such collateral substitutes to the MFI is based entirely on the moral enforcement vis-à-vis the borrower.

In practice though, very few MFIs go out of their ways to innovate in collateralisation: ABA in Egypt accepts post-dated checks, ADEMI in the Dominican Republic accepts a personal guarantee (co-signer) and moveable assets for smaller transactions, while for loans exceeding $40,000 proper collateral in the form of land, deeds are required. Indonesia's BRI, one of the largest MFIs worldwide and in many respects a pioneer, very conventionally insists on land titles or any other proof of asset ownership.

Some have blamed legal restrictions[14] for the reluctance of MFIs to improvise with collateral. The law also seems to be too slow to catch up with security transactions as they are handled in the informal economy. Others[15] claim that the lack of formal property rights is in fact the main cause for financial exclusion in most low-income countries. These informal assets would add up to US$10 trillion worldwide and could serve as collateral if only the actual status of possession and ownership was formalised. As this is not the case there is less funding of income generating activities than would otherwise be the case. Informality leads here to a suboptimal level of finance and investment.

Still, even where property registries exist this does not mean that they are used for collateralisation: the transaction costs involved in finding the right kind of registry, having to wait for the completion of the registration process, etc. can be prohibitive both for the lender (identifying, valuing, verifying, monitoring and liquidating security interests) and for the borrower (fees for documentation and tea money, working time and revenue foregone) (Table 5.4).

Table 5.4 Property registries in Tanzania[1]

Name and type of registrar	Responsible ministry	Location	Document registration	Collateralisation process	Repossession
Gen. admin. registries	Justice	District capitals	Less than one month	n.a.	Depends on court order
Register of business names	Home Affairs	Dar es Salaam	One to six months	n.a.	Depends on court order
Registrar of companies	Industry and Commerce	Dar es Salaam	One month	Less than three months	Depends on court order and bankruptcy law
Registry of motor vehicles	Finance	All districts	Less than a week	Less than three months	Depends on court order
Registry of land titles	Lands	Six zones	One to three months	Three to nine months	Depends on court order

[1] ILO, Securing Small Loans: the Transaction Costs of Taking Collateral, Report to the Donors' Working Group on Financial Sector Development, Social Finance Program, Geneva, (unpublished project document), February 2001.

38 *Methods and techniques*

Collateral substitutes are used in a legal vacuum. They are enforceable by informal, para legal or social means, but not in court. The effectiveness of joint liability or other collateral substitutes is moral, not legal.

Apart from that, collateral substitutes have only limited marketable value.[16] A second-hand refrigerator taken as security is unlikely to catch significant cash on the local market. Understandably many MFIs prefer to avoid experiments with collateral substitutes.[17] If MFIs use collateral substitutes at all, then actually less as stand-alone instruments rather than in combination with conventional collateral or – if this is not available – resort to internal means to exert moral pressure on the client. Prior savings is such a prodding technique. Clients are required to deposit upfront either a given amount of cash or/and make payments into an account for a minimum period of time with a given frequency, in many credit unions up to six months, with very strict terms of withdrawal.

Collateral substitution – where it is happening – tends to be reserved for smaller transactions and at the beginning of a client relationship. The substitute serves as a stepping stone and bridge for progressively larger transactions. The larger the loans, the more likely the use of conventional collateral. The performance of collateral substitutes in enforcing repayment is mixed. While the loan delinquency rates of solidarity groups compare favourably with individual lending,[18] research found also that the effectiveness of screening and sanctioning in informal pressure instruments weakens over time.[19]

Combining financial with non-financial services

Banks do not offer courses on functional literacy or safety and hygiene in sanitation. They do not demonstrate to their customers how to sterilise milk or how to use a cell phone to get information on market prices. Many MFIs, by contrast, do just that. For the MFI, these non-financial services come at a cost in the form of additional staff or subcontracts to a local NGO. MFI charge user fees, notably for business-related services, but even these cover rarely the full costs. For social services fees are simply not charged at all, like courses on maternal healthcare.[20] So, even with a good measure of cross subsidisation, non-financial services can be a burden to the MFI.

Coupling financial and non-financial services can yield risk-related information that pure lending would not produce. On the other hand, if a MFI gets too much involved in advising the client on her business, it might end up in a conflict of interest between its advisory and funding functions and be confronted with an unhappy client who considers herself poorly advised and hence under no obligation to pay back the loan.

Notes

1 A. Sen, The Political Economy of Targeting, World Bank Conference on Public Expenditures and the Poor: Incidence and Targeting, Washington, June 1992.
2 Coady International Institute, op. cit. pp. X–XII.
3 Ford Foundation, CGAP, EU and SPTF, Poverty Targeting and Measurement Tools in Microfinance, October 2010. The average costs for implementing the PPI is between $1,000 and $30,000 and for the PAT between $1,500 and $10,000. It takes 1–20 minutes to do a PPI survey per client and 10–40 minutes to do a PAT survey.
4 Micro Banking Bulletin, Issue No. 12, 2006.
5 World Bank, Targeting the Poor, Development Brief, number 9, February 1993.
6 A. Sen, op. cit., p. 3.
7 T. Besley and S. Coate, op. cit., p. 3.
8 S. Berenbach and D. Guzman, The Solidarity Group Experience, GEMINI WP 31, June 1992; M. Otero, A Question of Impact, Solidarity Group Programs and their Approach to Evaluation, PACT Publication, September 1989.
9 J. Stiglitz and A. Weiss, Asymmetric information in credit markets and its implication for macroeconomics, *Oxford Economic Papers*, vol. 44, 1992, pp. 694–724.
10 S. Berenbach et al., op. cit. pp. 41–42.
11 T. Besley and S. Coate, Group lending, repayment incentives and social collateral, *Journal of Development Economics*, vol. 46, 1995, p. 11.
12 T. Besley and S. Coate, op cit. p. 16
13 S. Berenbach et al., op. cit., p. 3; M. Goldberg and P. Hunte, Financial Services for the Poor: lessons on group-based models from 5 South NGOs, World Bank Asia Technical Department, 1995; J. Paxton et al., Modelling Group Loan Repayment Behaviour: new insights from Burkina Faso, Economic Development and Cultural Change, 2000, p. 640; M. J. Woolcock, Learning from Failures in Microfinance – what unsuccessful cases tell us about how group-based programs work, *American Journal of Economics and Sociology*, vol. 58, no. 1, January 1999, pp. 34–35.
14 H. Fleisig, Secured Transactions: the power of Collateral, Finance and Development June 1996; by the same author: The Power of Collateral, Viewpoint Note 43, World Bank, April 1995; idem, The Right to Borrow, Viewpoint 44, World Bank, April 1995; H. Fleisig et al., Legal Restrictions on Security Interests limit Access to Credit in Bolivia, *The International Lawyer*, vol. 31, no. 1, 1997; see also: www.ceal.org.
15 H.de Soto, *The Mystery of Capital: Why Capitalism Triumphs in the West and Fails Everywhere Else.* Basic Books, 2000.
16 B. Balkenhol and H. Schütte, Collateral, Collateral Law and Collateral Substitutes, Social Finance Program, Working Paper 26, ILO Geneva 2001, p. 14

40 *Methods and techniques*

17 As a survey of largely government-owned rural banks and MFIs in South East Asia showed: G. Llanto, B. Balkenhol and M. Zulfikli, Breaking Barriers to Formal Credit – Asian Experiences on collateral substitutes, APRACA/ILO/SDC, Bangkok, 1996 ....

18 R. Christen, E. Rhyne, and R. C. Vogel, Maximizing the outreach of microenterprise finance: the merging lessons of successful programs, USAID, 1995.

19 L. Bennett, The Necessity – and the Dangers – of Combining Social and Financial Intermediation to reach the Poor, Brookings Institution, Washington 1994; Sh. Yaqub, Empowered to default? Evidence from BRAC's micro-credit programmes, *SED*, vol. 6, 1995, pp. 4–13.

20 CGAP, Microfinance, Grants and non-financial responses to poverty reduction – where does microcredit fit? Focus Note 20, December 2002.

6 Microfinance institutions

"What actually is a microfinance *institution*?" There are several ways to provide financial services to the poor. Revolving loan funds or multipurpose development programmes with a financing mechanism do that, but they cannot be considered institutions, lacking specialisation and a certain permanency. An institutional approach to microfinance also implies some form of organised professionalism, like membership in representative associations, adherence to a commonly accepted set of good practices (like the Smart Campaign) on client protection and compliance with rules that licence, supervise and regulate financial intermediaries.[1]

Leaving aside revolving loan funds and other temporary set-ups for the distribution of very small loans, one is still left with a puzzling heterogeneity: microfinance institutions that differ in their internal and external formalisation. Some are registered with a government agency, the central bank or the bank supervisor and are therefore regularly supervised and audited to verify whether they comply with for instance prudential ratios.[2] Others are not. Many are in the process of obtaining an operating licence, and still others are in a regulatory limbo.

Any figure of the number of MFIs is necessarily guesswork. In the literature, one often finds the number 10,000, without an explanation how it is computed. In a 2004 paper[3] CGAP refers to over 3,000 AFIs ("alternative financial institutions"), a term encompassing MFIs proper (NGOs and non-bank financial institutions [NBFIs], microfinance banks, financial cooperatives, but also rural banks, state agricultural and development banks and postal savings banks). According to the "State of the Campaign Report 2015" of the Microcredit Summit Campaign[4] 3,098 microfinance institutions reported to the Campaign at the end of 2013 with over 210 million borrowers. In a blog in July 2013, CGAP mentions "more than 2,100 microfinance institutions" based on MIX data. Currently the MIX Market lists over 1,400 financial service providers in the South, i.e. MFIs that voluntarily submit information about their activities at the end of 2016.[5]

42   *Microfinance institutions*

Table 6.1 Microfinance institutions worldwide (MFIs on the MIX Market)

MIX 2017	Number	Clients (mio)	Loan portfolio ($1,000 mio)
Africa	369	6.4	8.34
East Asia	175	19.67	18.3
E. Europe and C. Asia	175	3.82	13.36
Latin America	421	24.79	46.05
MENA	38	2.42	1.54
South Asia	232	76.17	23.94
Global[1]	1,410	133.27	111.53

[1] Without Western Europe and North America.

These variations may be the result of different counting methods or due to the fact that fewer MFIs bother to report annually to the MIX, the Micro Credit Summit Campaign or other data collecting networks. It could also be evidence of the disappearance of MFIs from the market. Be that as it may, the exact number of MFIs and the evolution of that number over time are hard to determine. Suffice it to say that they are in their low thousands with some smaller ones closing down year after year, some growing on their own or through mergers and acquisitions and several changing their legal form.

Microfinance is a global phenomenon, with microfinance institutions operating in every region of the world,[6] however, mostly in Africa, Asia and Latin America (MIX Market and 2017) (Table 6.1).

Over the past five years up to 2017 the number of microfinance institutions reporting to the MIX Market has grown by 21%, the number of clients by 45% and the overall loan portfolios by 21%. Whatever may have been said about the demise of microfinance, these figures speak a different language. They are not those of an industry in decline.

Types

There are four main types of microfinance institutions:[7] NGOs, financial cooperatives, non-bank financial institutions and microfinance banks. Each type combines financial and social goals in a distinct manner. Although all committed to microfinance as a double bottom line business, the types of MFIs differ essentially by mission, ownership, access to resources and accessibility to clients.[8]

The following table shows the specific features of these types of MFIs. These features determine where exactly the type of MFI is positioned in the space between outreach to the poor and profitability.

Microfinance institutions 43

These features predispose to what extent a MFI is likely to stick to its double bottom line or drift to a more pronounced social or financial business model (Table 6.2).

Mission, ownership, ease of access to capital, proximity to clients and other features make MFIs more or less accessible for the population segments that they target, whether the ultra-poor, or household-enterprises near or above the poverty line, or microenterprises with a single income generating business or small formal, but un-bankable firms. The eligibility criteria differ, of course, not just with the types of institutions but also with the financial instruments. Rather than taking out a loan, poor households may prefer to have accessible, relatively liquid and remunerated deposit facilities or buy some crop insurance to minimize losses in case of floods or drought. Clients may also wish to have simple and rapid facilities to transfer or receive cash.

Not every type of MFI can offer deposits, insurance and payment services, only MFIs that are supervised and regulated. Paradoxically the type of MFI considered most poverty oriented – NGOs – cannot take deposits, which many consider to be the financial service most relevant to the poor. On the other hand, microfinance banks with their broader product offer and variety of services should in theory be attractive to the poor, but due to their business model tend to be geared more towards larger scale transactions.

Table 6.2 Features of different types of MFIs

	NGOs	*Cooperatives*	*Microfinance banks*	*Non-banking financial institutions*
Mission	Reduction of poverty	Service to members and local community	Promotion of micro- and small enterprises	Financial inclusion
Ownership	Remote and diffuse	Members are owners	Shareholders	Shareholders
Access to capital	Grants and soft loans	Member deposits; grants	Domestic capital market; depositors; donors, private investors	Domestic capital market; donors, private investors
Accessibility for clients	High	Restricted to members	Requirements on transaction size, collateral and formality	Requirements on transaction size, collateral and formality

44 *Microfinance institutions*

The four main types of microfinance institutions have their own distinct manner of combining profitability and outreach: NGOs have the strongest mission and mandate to work with the poor and vulnerable, and if they break even it is largely thanks to subsidies. Cooperatives have a clear mission to foster solidarity in a local community. A client of a savings and credit cooperative first has to join and buy member shares. Social outreach is limited to members. A financial cooperative is to maximize service to members – not its own profits. Microfinance banks obey a commercial business logic in the first place and accommodate outreach to the poor and unbanked to the extent possible. Lastly, non-banking financial institutions (NBFI) active in microfinance obey a commercial logic and are regulated like microfinance banks. In most countries, NBFI-MFIs occupy niche markets that allow small scale transactions, like equipment finance and leasing, housing finance, hire purchase and insurance brokerage. Because of regulatory reasons valid in some countries MFIs have opted for the status of NBFI to operate in the mainstream market and take deposits. Cambodia is a case in point.[9]

Within each type of MFI, one finds variations in the way financial and social goals are pursued. ACLEDA in Cambodia is a microfinance bank that seeks to "provide micro, small and medium entrepreneurs with the wherewithal to manage their financial resources efficiently and by doing so to improve the quality of their lives."[10] The average ACLEDA loan exceeds $6,000, which is very large in relation to average per capita income (687% of GNI per head). In 2016 its profitability stood at 3% RoA and 21% RoE. ACLEDA Bank stands apart, as there is no other MFI in Cambodia that has the legal form of a micro-bank.

The majority of MFIs in Cambodia are NBFIs. Even within this category, there are interesting differences from MFI to MFI: AMK sees as its mission "to help large numbers of poor people to improve their livelihood options through the delivery of appropriate and viable microfinance services."[11] This MFI has an average loan size of $464, which represents just 49% of GNI per head, while its RoA stood at 3.5% and its RoE at 20%. AMRET, another NBFI in Cambodia, seeks to "provide a wide range of financial services to low income people as well as micro, small and medium enterprises while achieving a high level of financial and social performance." It comes across as much more commercial with average loan sizes of $1,924 (= 202% of GNI per head) and profitability indicators of 4.35% RoA and 24.53% RoE.[12] So, not all NGO-MFIs are alike, and neither are all NBFI-MFIs nor all microfinance banks in their combination of social and commercial goals.

Microfinance institutions 45

In diversified microfinance markets the consumer normally has the choice between all four types, theoretically. For a poor household, what matters most are features like proximity, quick turnaround, flexible collateral requirements, understandable terms and a readiness to engage in small ticket sizes. A survey of four affiliates of the Women's World Banking (WWB) network revealed that "customers want higher loan amounts, faster turn-around times, lower loan requirements and lower prices."[13] They prefer individual loans over group loans and would like to see a greater diversity of financial products.

Looking at the relative strengths and weaknesses of the four main types of MFIs, none matches these client expectations exactly. NGOs may be relaxed about collateral, but they often insist on joint liability and group lending. Cooperatives allow for and even encourage savings, but they are not the fastest administrators of financial transactions. Microfinance banks have the full gamut of services but insist on some tangible form of collateral. This mixed picture explains why in most markets the four main types coexist more or less peacefully.

Seen through an institutional lens, in terms of profitability and efficiency, then NBFIs and financial cooperatives would seem to perform better than NGOs and microfinance banks (Table 6.3).[14]

Microfinance banks are the largest microfinance providers on average in terms of numbers of clients, far ahead of NBFIs, NGOs and cooperatives. The smallest loans on average are managed by NGOs, followed by NBFIs, microfinance banks and cooperatives. The strong social outreach of NGO type MFIs is confirmed if we relate the loan amount to GNI per head. Here NGO-MFIs come out clearly as most

Table 6.3 Indicators of financial and social performance by type of MFI

MBB 2006 data	MF banks	Cooperatives[1]	NBFIs	NGOs
Active borrowers (median)	62,385	7,910	17,728	13,868
Average loan balance per borrower ($)	1,215	1,518	808	297
Average loan balance per borrower/GNI per capita (%)	85	63	59	19
Profitability (OSS) (%)	112	111	125	117
Profitability (FSS) (%)	109	107	114	109
Efficiency (operating expense/ loan portfolio) (%)	19.6	14.4	17.9	27.1

[1] There are just 25 financial cooperatives in the overall sample of 340 MFIs. These 25 might not be representative of all financial cooperatives in the microfinance field: their small member numbers, high average loan balance and extremely good efficient measures could be the consequence.

46 Microfinance institutions

Table 6.4 Financial performance of MFIs by charter type (2009–2016)

The MIX 2017[1]	Microfinance banks	Financial cooperatives	NBFIs	NGOs
Loan portfolio average annual growth rate (%)	23.4	29.4	34.8	29.4
PAR 90 average[2]	2.7	4.1	2.2	2.2
Write-off ratio	0.9	0.5	1.0	0.7
Return on equity	10.4	5.8	7.3	9.3

[1] Quoted from Lehigh U. op. cit., p. 11.
[2] To put this into perspective: the average median annual PAR 90 of all banks worldwide was 3.9%!

poverty-oriented. Comparing the different types of MFIs, one finds – surprisingly – that microfinance banks are not significantly more profitable than NGOs. In terms of efficiency, cooperatives come out best, followed by NBFIs, micro-banks and NGOs (Table 6.4).

Performance of microfinance institutions

When is a microfinance institution a *good* microfinance institution? What makes MFI X better than MFI Y? To measure quality, there is a host of possible criteria: the value of savings mobilized, number of savings accounts, average balance on deposits, or one could look at the overall value of the loan portfolio, number of loans extended, average value of loans, annual real growth of assets, % of poor actually reached, the return on assets, the operating costs per client, the number of branches, the proportion of women reached and many more. While some researchers value indicators of outreach more highly and others tend to emphasize more the financials of the institution, there is a broad and stable consensus that the performance of a microfinance institution cannot be appreciated exclusively in terms of outreach *or* profitability.

When Forbes published in 2007 a ranking of the best performing microfinance institutions[15] it seemed a breakthrough of microfinance into the mainstream world of finance and banking. However, a closer look revealed a fundamental misunderstanding of the nature microfinance. The ranking was based on scale, efficiency, risk and returns, all plausible criteria but purely financial. What the Forbes article missed out on was the social dimension of microfinance performance, i.e. the relation of a MFI to its clients, its outreach. Social performance is just as much part and parcel of institutional performance in microfinance as financial performance. What the Forbes ranking ignored were criteria such as how many poor households are reached, how poor they were, how many clients were women, how many lived in rural areas and so on. In short, the particularity of institutional performance in microfinance is that it is in two dimensions: financial and social.

Before addressing the tricky question how to synthesize the performance findings into single values, we briefly examine financial and social performance separately.

Financial performance

In terms of financial performance, MFIs are not very different from banks and other commercial financial service providers: productivity, efficiency, profitability and portfolio quality[16] are the criteria looked at. Each criterion has its standard indicators: portfolio quality is measured by the ratio of portfolio at risk in arrears at 30, 60 and 90 days/loan portfolio, the ratio of provisions for loan losses/loan portfolio or the write-off ratio. Similarly, productivity and efficiency are assessed with indicators taken from the standard financial management handbook. Profitability is equally measured by conventional indicators like return on assets, return on equity and the gross profit margin.

There is only one aspect in the measurement of financial performance where microfinance differs from conventional finance: the use of a twin indicators of profitability that sheds light on the prevalence subsidies. In addition to conventional measures of profitability, analysts of microfinance also use "OSS" and "FSS." OSS ("operational self-sufficiency") is a ratio of operational income and operational expenses; FSS ("financial self-sufficiency") adjusts the OSS for subsidies, inflation and accounting errors. This pair of profitability indicators corrects for the distortions due to subsidies channelled to microfinance institutions. OSS simply signals whether a MFI covers its costs and generates a surplus regardless of whether the revenue was generated by its own activities or whether some external partner injected substantial grants into the MFI. An OSS with a value of 100 or more signals that the MFIs is not incurring losses. Clearly the OSS by itself does not tell the whole story. Practically all microfinance institutions benefit from subsidies, some more, some less. In fact, many MFIs continue to be subsidized in some implicit way often 10 years after having been set up.[17] So, the "OSS" by itself would not give a realistic picture of an institution's actual capacity to survive in the market should subsidies be discontinued all of a sudden. In order to correct for a possible over-optimistic representation of a MFI's profitability, it is necessary to recalculate

48 *Microfinance institutions*

and adjust the OSS by taking into account real market resource costs. This way one gets a more realistic idea of the profitability and financial performance of a MFI: the financial self-sufficiency ratio, "FSS." A MFI that operates with resources on market terms and generates a surplus is genuinely sustainable. Or, as Woller and Schreiner put it: "financial self-sufficiency is the non-profit equivalent of profitability."[18]

Social performance

In contrast to financial performance, social performance of microfinance institutions is much more difficult to measure. There is not a canon of indicators of social performance, although the industry has made big strides towards a consensus.[19] Social performance measurement proposes to capture the "social worth" or outreach of what a MFI offers to its clients. Outreach can be looked at from several angles:[20] number of poor clients reached, poverty level, costs to the client, continuous local presence and range of products on offer.

In the early years of microfinance these aspects of outreach were not systematically examined. MFIs largely improvised in their social performance management. Social performance was equated with outreach, and that in turn was equated with the number of clients. Subsequently and with more and more probing questions put by donor agencies, other metrics were used that were easy to calculate and extract from MFI records: average loan or deposit amounts in terms of GNI per head, percentage of women clients or clients in rural areas. More ambitious, time-consuming and costly are systematic instruments to determine the level of poverty and other ambitious aspects of outreach, like the "Progress out of Poverty Index (PPI)"[21] or the "Poverty Assessment Tool (PAT)."[22]

Based on earlier work by M. Schreiner and G. Woller USAID presented in 2005 a conceptual framework to the notion "outreach."[23] It distinguished between six dimensions: (1) worth of outreach, defined as the client's willingness to pay, (2) cost of outreach, defined as the sum of price and non-price transaction costs, (3) depth of outreach (level of poverty), (4) breadth of outreach, defined by the number of clients, (5) length of outreach, defined as the time frame of supply of products and services, and (6) scope of outreach, defined as the number of distinct types of products and services supplied. These dimensions deal with the costs and stability of the relations with clients, counting and describing them, but they still stop short of tracking impact, i.e. changes at the level of the household or enterprise that can be attributed to the use of services and products provided by the MFI (see Chapter 11 on impact).

Still, the measurement of social performance did not live up to this ambitious conceptual framework. For example, in a 2008 ranking of the 100 "best" MFIs, the MIX Market[24] used as outreach criteria the absolute number of clients, the growth of that figure, market penetration and the provision of deposit accounts but not depth of outreach, length, scope, costs and worth.

It was not until 2011 that the Social Performance Task Force and the MIX Market jointly developed a list of 11 social performance indicators[25] on which MFIs were invited to report. Nine of these relate to institution-internal features (mission, governance, declaration on social responsibility to clients and the environment, range of products and services, financial and non-financial, human resources and staff incentives) or aspects in the relation between MFI and client (transparency in the costs of services, client retention and outreach by lending methodologies).

Currently MFIs report their social performance to the MIX Market[26] in terms of

- Number of active borrowers (total and by gender and location)
- Number of loans outstanding
- Average loan balance per borrower/GNI per head
- Number of depositors
- Number of deposit accounts
- Average deposit balance per depositor/GNI per head

While substantial progress has been made over the past 20 years to arrive at common criteria, measurement and reporting methods on social performance, a conceptual framework that captures all beneficial and damaging effects for clients is and will continue to be work in progress. In 2012, the Social Performance Task Force launched the Universal Standards for Social Performance Management ("the Universal Standards"), a "comprehensive manual of best practices to help financial service providers put clients at the center."[27]

So, clearly the focus in reporting on social performance has widened from the six aspects of outreach of 1999 to the Universal Standards of 2016. Consumer protection is new, and issues in connection with employees are new. By contrast, there is less emphasis on managing and reporting about depth, length, scope, costs and worth of outreach. These tricky aspects of outreach seem to lend themselves more to in-depth studies, rating exercises and institutional monographs. Standard, recurrent reporting on the social performance of MFIs, as for example to the MIX Market, thus captures only part of the story.

50   *Microfinance institutions*

Performance in microfinance: commercialisation

Microfinance markets are in constant flux: some institutions grow, others flounder and disappear, and many change their business model and approach over time in response to competition and changes in legal form and ownership. As a consequence, the exact position of a microfinance institution in the space between profitability and outreach is likely to change constantly. The following three sections look at common scenarios that change the combination of financial and social performance in a microfinance institution: commercialisation, transformation and mission drift. First, commercialisation.

There is nothing wrong with microfinance institutions seeking to establish themselves permanently in the local market and to remain responsive to their clients. It is normal that they seek a reasonable measure of profitability. It is even beneficial for the poor if the MFI grows, diversifies its sources of capital, becomes independent of donors, innovates in products and seeks to cut costs as long as it remains focused on the clientele for which it has declared to have a mission. If that is the meaning of commercialisation, then one wonders what the fuss was all about in the heated debates of the 1990s and 2000s about the direction that microfinance was taking.

But presumably M. Yunus had something else in mind when he declared "commercialization ... to be ... a terrible wrong turn for microfinance."[28] In the aftermath of IPOs of Compartamos in Mexico and SKS in India, Yunus saw commercialisation as the takeover of the ownership of microfinance institutions by external investors and an exclusive focus on profitability. Commercialisation would, in his perspective, be the departure from the original double bottom line that has been the landmark of microfinance.

Has that actually happened? Not in the case of Compartamos Banco.[29] Following its IPO in April 2007 its social performance actually became better, whether measured in terms of average loan amount per borrower (which decreased from 440 in 2006 to 415 in 2016) or in terms of the same ratio expressed in % of GNI per head (down from the already very low level of 4.76% [2006] to 3.52% [2016]). Moreover, Compartamos Banco started to offer deposit facilities in 2011, which by their modest average balance ($ 94) and take-up by close to 600,000 clients reached the poor. The only aspect that can be interpreted as a negative consequence of the IPO is the declining percentage of women clients, from 98.3% in 2006 to 87.4% in 2016.

While the four types of MFIs have distinct propensities towards social outreach or profitability, their relative positioning in the space of

Microfinance institutions 51

financial and social performance is not cast in stone. It changes over time and in relation to other MFIs. An NGO type of MFI can over time become "commercial," if that is understood to mean cost-covering prices and generate some profit, to position itself in relation to other MFIs in the local financial market, competitors and strategic partners. Going "commercial" can also imply to embrace regulation as a condition for growth and diversification. All these changes do not necessarily mean that the MFI leaves behind its original customers – but it can mean that.

Commercialisation can be analysed through a strictly institutional lens or by looking at all MFIs in a region or a country and track whether over time on average the combination of social and financial goals changed. In Latin America, for example,

> microfinance used to be the exclusive domain of non-profit organizations and cooperative societies. Today, commercial banks provide 29 percent of the funds that go to microenterprises. Non-governmental organizations (NGOs) that have transformed themselves into licensed financial institutions, together with other specially licensed financial intermediaries, provide another 45 percent.[30]

Why do MFIs then take a more commercial approach? Sometimes, it is donor partners or investors that push a MFI to become more commercial. Increasing competition and market saturation can also reinforce the tendency to look more rigorously at costs and prices (see Chapter 9). Commercialisation can also be the unintended result of public policy, like interest rate ceilings (see Chapter 10 Public Policy).

Commercialisation is likely to lead to mission drift. Indeed, when NGOs decide to become regulated microfinance institutions, it turns out that they tend to "provide larger loans to their clients than do unregulated NGOs."[31] On closer scrutiny, however, this does not necessarily mean that these MFIs replace their former, poorer customers by newer and better-off customers. It could be that the average demand for loans of these clients grew in response to the MFI's new strategy.[32]

Transformation

Commercialisation can – but must not – pass via transformation, while transformation inversely can end up in a more commercial approach of the MFI. Transformation of a microfinance institution means that it adopts a different legal and regulatory status.[33] MFIs transform from NGOs to NBFIs or micro-banks, rarely to cooperatives; in the

52 *Microfinance institutions*

opposite direction there is little transformation: no micro-bank has been observed to turn into a NGO. Not all MFIs that become more commercial change their legal personality, but in many cases a MFI that has undergone a transformation emerges with a different mix of social and financial goals. Transformation affects the entire MFI and its activities. It implies having to adjust to control by more and different stakeholders, to recruit staff with different skill profiles and to adapt to the new and unfamiliar compliance requirements.[34]

In almost all instances, the aim is to broaden and diversify the resource base, in particular to be able to collect deposits. This enhances the appeal of a MFI to clients, lowers its resource costs and removes an important obstacle to growth. The ability to collect deposits depends on the authorisation by a bank supervisor. A MFI's decision to transform is also motivated by the wish to spread the ownership (including to its own employees)[35], become eligible for partnerships with mobile banking agencies and fin-techs and broaden the range of products and services on offer. Obviously, these motivations are primarily geared to improve the MFI's financial performance, even if its clients are claimed to indirectly benefit, as well.

The effects of transformation on the double bottom line are mixed: if one takes ownership by private investors as the key indicator of commercialisation then transformation does not seem to have led the MFIs astray: "neither in Latin America nor in Asia has transformation led to a substantial increase in equity holding by commercial investors."[36] However, if one takes changes in the key indicators of outreach to the poor, i.e. average loan size, then transformation appears to have led to reduced social performance: "in 10 out of 12 transformed MFIs did the average loan size per client ratio increase, in 2 it decreased."[37]

Two instances of transformations, ACLEDA and Bancosol, show that in real life there is not simply a change in the legal form that is at stake, but the balance of financial imperatives and social benefits. Both MFIs started out as NGOs and transformed into micro-banks, **ACLEDA** in Cambodia and **Bancosol** in Bolivia.

ACLEDA is the largest provider of microfinance in Cambodia, and it has grown to be the largest commercial bank of the country: at the end of 2015, it held 43% of the country's microfinance portfolios ($2.4 billion) and 20% of the assets held by all financial institutions. 12% of customers using microfinance in Cambodia deal with it.[38] ACLEDA started out in 1993 as an NGO under the auspices of two international organisations, ILO and UNDP. It obtained the commercial banking licence in 2003, after five years of a conversion programme. In the course of conversion and as a result of its repositioning as a SME

Microfinance institutions   53

lender, several non-financial services were discontinued that used to be addressed at the poor: vocational training programmes for the poor, women empowerment and client tracking programmes. The majority of ACLEDA shares is currently held by the former NGO and the ACLEDA staff association.

The transformation did not come about without some change in the positioning in the market: whereas ACLEDA was initially targeted at the poor and unbanked, its current mission is small and medium enterprises.[39] This shift in focus is reflected in outreach: before the transformation in 2002, the average loan amount was $325, while in 2015 it was $6,009. The average loan balance per client expressed as a % of gross national income was inferior to 100 before 2002, which meant that ACLEDA catered effectively to poor people compared to the national average. In 2015 this ratio exceeded 600, i.e. the institution was dealing now with better off, middle-class clients having more important funding needs.[40] Interestingly, the profitability of ACLEDA has not dramatically improved as a result of the transformation, measured in terms of the operational self-sufficiency (unadjusted for subsidies and inflation). In 1999 the OSS of ACLEDA stood at 146%, and in 2015 it improved slightly to 154%.

Bancosol is the largest MFI in Bolivia in terms of numbers of clients (251,000 in a country with over 1.2 million clients of MFIs). In terms of loan portfolio size, it is the third largest with $1,174 billion after Banco Fassil and Banco FIE.[41] Bancosol transformed in 1991 from an NGO named PRODEM to Banco Solidario. Within a year the number of borrowers doubled, as did the average amount of loans and the number of loans disbursed. On the other hand, the financial situation did not spectacularly improve as Bancosol no longer received grants. Revenue from financial services remained roughly unchanged, as costs of funds went up, offsetting the reductions in cutting overheads (Table 6.5).

Table 6.5 Transformation: implications for funding costs and overheads

PRODEM/BANCOSOL	1991	1992	1993	1994
Revenue from lending	34	34	34	29
Grants	4	0	0	0
Total revenues	40	39	36	32
Staff expenses	13	18	12	10
Administration	8	8	5	4
Total operat. exp.	27	31	21	18
Cost of funds	4	6	13	12
Total expenses	37	36	35	30

54 *Microfinance institutions*

In 2015 the average loan amount expressed as a % of GNI was 183%,[42] up from 113% in 1999. Its operational self-sufficiency was 132% in 2015, compared to 107% in 1999.[43] Roughly speaking, following its transformation Bancosol has over the years moved up-market, not dramatically as in the case of ACLEDA, but slowly. At the same time, it has not turned into a purely commercially oriented microfinance institution. Bancosol has on the whole maintained its market position and mission, while ACLEDA changed its target market and business model. In conclusion transformation does not necessarily entail a more commercial positioning of a MFI.

Mission drift

The claim of microfinance is to reach out to the poor and change their lives for the better and at the same time build robust, sustainable financial service providers making a business out of it, a social business. The claim amounts to saying that it is possible to harmonize profits and social benefits – which intuitively would seem mutually exclusive.[44] Hardly surprising that research on institutions and markets in microfinance often focuses on the "trade-off" between financial and social performance.[45] In other words: for institutions intent to cover their costs and generate a profit, are they automatically obliged to discontinue some services to the poor, raise interest rates and close outlets in rural areas? Inversely: is outreach to very poor clients in remote areas necessarily at the expense of the institution's overall profitability? Or is there some way to transcend the trade-off? If an institution decides to change its business model and become marginally more commercial or inversely more client-centred, then is this necessarily at the expense of outreach to the poor or to its profitability? According to Cull et al. *"the global evidence shows that it is hard to do all things simultaneously. In practice, microfinance often entails distinct trade-offs between meeting social goals and maximizing financial performance."*[46] Intuitively, this would make sense in light of the marginal transaction costs and risks involved in expanding a portfolio of small loans to vulnerable clients in remote areas. Paxton sums up her literature review by saying that the *"deeper the outreach to underserved clients, the more reliant the institution is on subsidies."*[47]

On the other hand, a study of 11 microfinance programmes promoted by USAID found that there was *"no evidence of a direct trade-off between outreach, either deep or extensive and financial viability. The two goals are clearly not in opposition."*[48] Two conditions, in particular, seem to be required: scale and scope for cross-subsidisation. Paxton finds that banks and credit unions are able to reach down to poor clients because of economies of scale in the delivery of services and the possibility to offset losses in one section of the portfolio by surpluses in another.[49] NGOs, for their part, can improve on their financial performance without abandoning their client base, simply by becoming more efficient.

Mission drift[50] occurs as a result of many causes: a decision to transform, a deliberate push by donors and investors or a gradual slide towards more commercialisation. It can happen as the consequence of increased competition with other MFIs. Interest rate caps and other public policy measures can also push a MFI to deviate from its original double bottom line, away from outreach to the poor towards a greater emphasis on profitability. Whether or not mission drift occurs depends on the strength of its commitment to social mission, on governance and ownership of the MFI, on the return expectations of shareholders and whether the MFI's donor partners cancel each other out in their prodding of the MFI towards more social or more financial performance.[51]

One way to avoid mission drift is to become more efficient. Recent studies by N. Hermes et al., R. Mersland and R. O. Strom and R. Cull et al. found that MFIs that control their costs better may not automatically improve their profitability – adjusted for subsidies, but their efficiency gains can benefit poor clients. In other words, MFIs can avoid the trap of mission drift by improving their efficiency. Some profitable MFIs are inefficient and can afford to remain so because they enjoy a monopoly or receive massive subsidies. Other MFIs are efficient without quite being profitable. Efficiency does not guarantee profitability, but it allows a MFI to improve its performance along its original double bottom line.

The empirical evidence of a trade-off and subsequent mission drift is mixed.[52] According to Cull et al. the lending methodology appears to make a difference: MFIs that use an individual lending approach are more likely to undergo mission drift compared to MFIs that continue to work with groups. If a move to larger average loan sizes is accompanied by cost-cutting measures, then mission drift can be avoided: the initial balance between social and financial goals is maintained. Reviewing 435 MFIs over a 10-year period, Hermes et al. find "rather a strong evidence for a trade-off between outreach to the poor and efficiency of MFIs."[53] Mersland and Strom reviewed 379 MFIs in 74 countries and find little evidence of mission drift. While it "may occur if an MFI seeks higher financial returns, this effect is

56 *Microfinance institutions*

neutralized if the MFI is more cost efficient."[54] Higher efficiency can help avoid mission drift. Even commercialisation does not always seem to be detrimental to the poor: a study of the microfinance market in Uganda by Darko concludes that "commercialisation provides MFIs the opportunity to apply good banking principles and by so doing attract funds from commercial sources or are able to diversify their services."[55]

Towards a single metric

A unified measure of the overall institutional performance of a microfinance institution has to be constructed. Rating agencies, for example, whose business it is to examine MFI from all angles, attach weights to the different dimensions of institutional performance: governance and management, financial performance, human resources, internal controls and audits, client protection and other aspects of social performance.[56] Rating agencies have their own philosophy in this regard or follow the priorities of the institutions mandating them. Logically there is a good dose of subjectivity in how the financial and social dimensions of performance are brought together and harmonized in a single measure.

Fortunately, the microfinance field has collected such a wealth of data about thousands of institutions that it is possible to relate the performance of a given individual MFI to a "peer group" of similar MFIs. The Micro Banking Bulletin[57] developed a framework of parameters that facilitate performance assessment of MFIs by differentiating MFIs by

- Legal form
- Location
- Scale of operations already attained (measured as the size of gross loan portfolio)
- Target markets (average loan balance as % of GDP per capita)
- Lending methodology (group, individual lending, mixed)
- Level of country income

To illustrate: an NGO-MFI operating in a remote part of a Sahel economy reaching out to very poor clients via group lending can be compared in terms of efficiency to other NGO-MFIs operating in comparable locations with a similar approach. By contrast it does not make sense to compare its efficiency to a microfinance bank like ACLEDA. There is no absolute value of efficiency, a given MFI is more or less efficient in relation to

Microfinance institutions 57

comparable MFIs. The MBB list of factors allows the construction of "peer groups" of similar microfinance institutions. Within a peer group there is always one MFI that combines profitability and outreach to the poor more efficiently than the others, as the figure that follows illustrates (Figure 6.1).[58]

The trick is how narrowly to define peer groups: taking simply the legal form as the defining criterion would result in too large – and heterogeneous – peer groups. On the other hand, one does not want the peer groups to be too narrowly drawn, applying a long list of criteria and then end up with just a handful of similar MFIs. The advantage of putting together similarly constituted MFIs in peer groups is that one does not need to disentangle the real or imagined trade-offs between social impact and financial performance. The respective mix of these two goals is taken as given and what counts as performance is purely the efficiency with which similar MFIs use inputs to produce outputs, social *and* financial.

What differentiates MFIs belonging to the same peer group is how efficiently they transform "inputs," i.e. the number and per head cost of staff, costs of financial resources and overheads into outputs, for example number of loan or deposit accounts, number of clients, gross yield, etc. In every peer group some MFIs are more efficient than

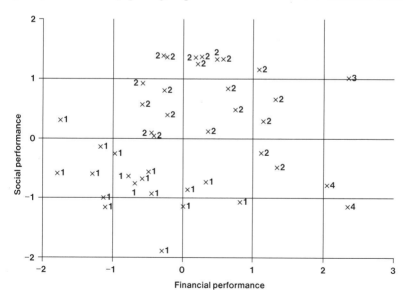

Figure 6.1 Scatter gram: scores and clusters.

others, and there is always one MFI that extracts the maximum outputs out of its inputs or uses the least inputs for a given level of outputs (Figures 6.2 and 6.3).

Flückiger and Vassiliev[59] measured the performance of MFIs in Peru on the basis of their relative efficiency, i.e. in relation to the best MFI in the respective three peer groups, "cajas municipales," "cajas rurales" and NGO-MFIs ("Edpymes"). The 40 MFIs reviewed consisted of 14 in the first peer group, 12 in the second and 14 in the third. The study used as input variables staff, assets and operating expense and as output variables the number and volume of loans as well as net operating income. In each of the three peer groups, they identified one MFI as "best in class": Camco Piura in the NGO peer group, CRAC Cajamarca in the group of Cajas Rurales and CMAC Trujillo in the peer group of Cajas Municipales. By working on their efficiency all the other 37 MFIs can expect to improve both social and financial performance without a trade-off or mission drift, without transforming and without abandoning their double bottom line.

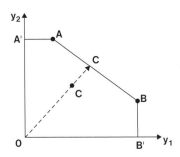

Figure 6.2 Best practice frontier in two output coordinates.

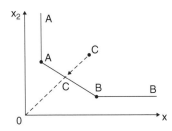

Figure 6.3 Best practice frontier in two input coordinates.

Notes

1 Another feature of this emerging specialisation and professionalisation are collective bargaining frameworks adopted in some countries to bring some order in employment relations and address sector-wide problems like inter-institutional poaching of staff: www.apsfdsenegal.com.

2 The PARMEC law in the West African Monetary Union, for example, lists the following ratios that the supervised entities need to comply with: the MFI may not distribute to a single client more than 10% of the entire loan portfolio; the MFI managers may not get more than 20% of the entire loan portfolio; 15% of the annual surplus must be ploughed back into the reserves and the total risk exposure must not exceed the double of the deposits managed.

3 CGAP, Financial Institutions with a Double Bottom Line – Implications for the future of Microfinance, Occasional Papers 8, July 2004.

4 https://stateofthecampaign.org/data-reported/

5 www.themix.org/mixmarket

6 Even in high-income countries, although they are very few and small (see EMN Overview Reports).

7 We do not consider here commercial banks that open a microfinance window. We also do not look at government-sponsored retail mechanisms like funds.

8 Public sector MFIs are postal savings banks and municipal savings banks.

9 Point made by Daniel Rozas.

10 www.acledabank.com.kh/

11 www.amkcambodia.com/

12 The figures are from the MIXMARKET.

13 WWB, What do microfinance customers value?, New York, 2002.

14 The MBB Trend lines study collected data from 340 MFIs over the period 2004–2006: 138 NGOs, 131 NBFIs, 29 microfinance banks, 25 financial cooperatives and 16 rural banks.

15 www.forbes.com/2007/12/20/microfinance-philanthropy-credit-biz-cz_ms_1220microfinance_table_2.html

16 CGAP, Microfinance Consensus Guidelines – Definitions of selected financial terms, ratios and adjustments for microfinance, 2003.

17 R. Cull, A. Demirguc-Kunt, and J. Morduch, The Microfinance Business Model – Enduring Subsidy and Modest Profit, Policy Research Working Paper 7786, World Bank Development Research Group, August 2016.

18 G. Woller and M. Schreiner, Poverty Lending, Financial Self Sufficiency and the six Aspects of Outreach, SEEP Network, 2004, p. 1.

19 Thanks to the Social Performance Task Force, a global membership organisation started in 2006 that works to advance social performance management and its cooperation with the MIX Market.

20 S. Navajas et al., Microcredit and the poorest of the poor: theory and evidence from Bolivia, *World Development*, vol. 28, no. 2, 2000, pp. 333–346.

21 www.progressoutofpoverty.org/ and

22 www.povertytools.org/

23 G. Woller and Chemonics for USAID, Proposal for a social performance measurement framework in microfinance: the six aspects of outreach, Micro REPORT #26, July 2005.

60 Microfinance institutions

24 MIX Market, The 2008 MIX Global 100 Composite Rankings of Microfinance Institutions, A report from the Microfinance Information Exchange, Inc. (MIX) December, 2008.

25 https://sptf.info/component/content/article?id=120:mix-sp-indicators

26 For example, for Vision Fund in Cambodia: https://reports.themix.org/mfi/visionfund-cambodia

27 https://sptf.info/universal-standards-for-spm/universal-standards. Version 2.0 of the SPTF Universal Standards of 2016 consist of six areas of performance: (1) Define and Monitor Social Goals. (2) Ensure Board, Management, and Employee Commitment to Social Goals. (3) Design Products, Services, and Delivery Channels that Meet Clients' Needs and Preferences. (4) Treat Clients Responsibly. (5) Treat Employees Responsibly. (6) Balance Financial and Social Performance.

28 Quoted in D. Roodman, op. cit., p. 331.

29 The figures are from the MIX Market.

30 CGAP, COMMERCIALIZATION AND MISSION DRIFT – THE TRANSFORMATION OF MICROFINANCE IN LATIN AMERICA, Occasional Paper 5, 2001, p. 1.

31 CGAP, op. cit., p. 13.

32 CGAP, op. cit., p. 16.

33 N. Fernando, Micro success story? Transformation of NGOs into regulated financial institutions, ADB, June 2004, p. 2.

34 J. Ledgerwood and V. White, op. cit., p. 68.

35 J. Ledgerwood and V. White, Transforming Microfinance Institutions - Providing Full Financial Services to the Poor, World Bank, 2006, p. 207: K-REP, CARDBANK, ADEMI.

36 N. Fernando, op. cit., pp. 8 and 10.

37 N. Fernando, op. cit. p. 22.

38 www.themix.org.

39 www.acledabank.com.kh: "Our mission is to provide micro, small and medium entrepreneurs with the wherewithal to manage their financial resources efficiently and by doing so to improve the quality of their lives."

40 https://reports.themix.org/mfi/acleda

41 https://www.themix.org/mixmarket/countries-regions/bolivia

42 https://reports.themix.org/mfi/bancosol

43 https://reports.themix.org/mfi/bancosol

44 F. Bedecarrats and C. Lapenu, Assessing microfinance: striking the balance between social utility and financial performance, in: *Microfinance in Developing Countries - Issues, Policies and Performance Evaluation*, Palgrave McMillan, 2013, pp. 62–82.

45 R. Cull, A. Demirgüç-Kunt, and J. Morduch, Microfinance Trade-offs - Regulation, Competition, and Financing, Policy Research Working Paper 5086, The World Bank Development Research Group, Finance and Private Sector Team, October 2009.

46 R. Cull et al., op. cit., p. 17.

47 J. Paxton, Depth of outreach and its relation to the sustainability of microfinance institutions, *Savings and Development*, XXVI, no. 1, 2002, p. 78.

48 Robert Peck Christen, Elisabeth Rhyne, Robert C. Vogel and Cressida McKean, Maximizing the Outreach of Microenterprise Finance – An Analysis of Successful Microfinance Programs, USAID, July 1995, op. cit.,

Microfinance institutions 61

p. 33, 27. However, it should be noted that the finding cannot be really surprising since the programmes selected were all relatively large and financially well-performing MFIs.

49 J. Paxton, op. cit., pp. 79–80.

50 Defined simply as "*a tendency ...to extend larger average loan sizes in the process of scaling-up*" B. Armendariz and A. Szafarz, On Mission Drift in MFIs, p. 341 in *The Handbook of Microfinance*, Singapore, 2011.

51 G. Woller, The promise and peril of microfinance commercialization, *Small Enterprise Development*, vol. 13, no. 4, 2002, p. 19.

52 See N. Hermes, R. Lensink, and A. Meesters, *Outreach and Efficiency of Microfinance Institutions*, Centre for International Banking, Insurance and Finance (CIBIF), University of Groningen, 2007; R. Cull, A. Demirguç-Kunt, and J. Morduch, Financial performance and outreach: a global analysis of leading microbanks, *Economic Journal, Royal Economic Society*, vol. 117, no. 517, 2007; pp. 107–F133, B. Gutiérrez-Nieto, C. Serrano-Cinca, and C. Mar Molinero, Social efficiency in microfinance institutions, *Journal of Operational Research Society*, vol. 60, 2009, pp. 104–119.
Other research papers on this issue are identified in P. Engels, Mission Drift in Microfinance, the influence of institutional and country risk indicators on the trade-off between the financial and social performance of microfinance institutions, Tilburg University October 2009.

53 N. Hermes, et al., op. cit., p. 16.

54 R. Mersland and R.O. Strom, Microfinance mission drift?, *World Development*, vol. 38, no. 1, January 2010, p. 31.

55 F. A. Darko, Is there a mission drift in microfinance? Op. cit., p. 21.

56 Rating Guide, Volume 1: The Microfinance Institutional Rating, The Rating Initiative, October 2012, p. 7.

57 MicroBanking Bulletin (MBB), no. 9, July 2003.

58 G. Ferro Luzzi and S. Weber, Measuring the performance of MFIs: an application of factor analysis, in: B. Balkenhol (ed.), *Microfinance and Public Policy*, op. cit., p. 164.

59 Y. Flückiger and A. Vassiliev, Efficiency in microfinance institutions: an application of data envelopment analysis to MFIs in Peru, in: B. Balkenhol (ed.), *Microfinance and Public Policy*, Palgrave Macmillan/ILO, 2007, p. 95.

7 Investing in microfinance

The preceding chapter showed how microfinance institutions seek to strike a balance between financial results and benefits for their clients, each institution having its own particular approach. In the following two chapters the focus will be on two external factors that can tip the balance one way or another: investments and subsidies.

Investors in financial markets go for a return, whether that is a capital gain or dividends or interest; the benefit is financial, and the investee just has to produce a reasonable return on investment. This is not so in microfinance. It is true that MFIs generate profits or incur losses. In that respect, MFIs are like other investee firms. But financial performance is only half the story – the other half is effects on clients, i.e. social performance. The hybrid nature of MFIs makes them attractive for all sorts of investors. Commercially oriented investors will approach MFIs exclusively from an angle of profitability, just as social investors will be primarily guided by their impact on the poor – often disregarding the other dimension. In all likelihood, though, investors that take an interest in microfinance are conscious of the double bottom line, characteristic of microfinance. They want to get the best of two worlds. They are prepared to tolerate a less than maximum financial return as long as there is some social impact. Most investors active in the field of microfinance want their MFIs to strike a reasonable balance between these two goals.

Still, not all investors have the same view of what this balance should look like in a given MFI. As it happens the market for investments in microfinance is organised in a diverse range of funds that allows every type of investor to pick and choose a fund with a portfolio of MFIs to his/her liking. Commercial investors can select a vehicle that promises high returns, whilst social investors or philanthropists go for funds with a positive, but moderate financial return and some evidence of social impact. This market for investments in microfinance is organised by "Microfinance Investment Vehicles" (MIVs) serving as intermediaries between retail investors and microfinance institutions (investees).[1]

Microfinance started to attract the interest of investors in the late 1990s. It was then that MIVs were created to channel cross-border investments from the North to the South.[2] By 2017, the number of MIVs has grown to over 100. A recent survey by Symbiotics lists 93 documented microfinance investment vehicles (MIVs)[3] out of a total of 127. Globally assets under management by these MIVs were $12.6 billion as of December 2016. Over the past 10 years, this volume has quintupled. Investments in microfinance come from different sources, private and institutional, i.e. pension funds, insurances (52%), public (20%), high net worth individuals (4%) and retail investors (24%). These investments into MFIs are made predominantly in the form of debt (82%). Equity-only funds make up 16% of MIV investments.

The relation between the type of investor and the kind of investment fund is shown in the graph that follows (Figure 7.1)[4].

Two-thirds of MIV investment goes to MFIs in Eastern Europe/Central Asia and Latin America/Caribbean. The five largest MIVs

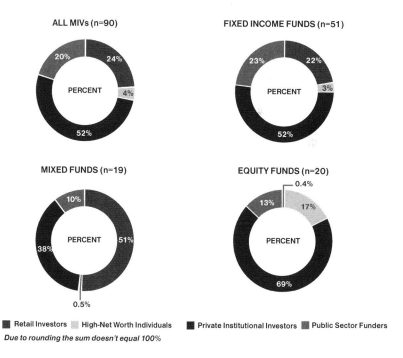

Figure 7.1 Types of investors and types of funds.

64 *Investing in microfinance*

account for 38% of the total in 2016 and the 10 largest for 56%. MIVs prefer larger MFIs as investees: the largest microfinance institutions, those with over $100 million in assets, are the destination of 58% of MIV investments, while 36% go to MFIs with assets between $10 and 100 million and only 6% are destined to MFIs with assets of less than $10 million. The average MIV debt instrument amounts to $2.1 million and has a maturity of two to three years. In 2016 MIVs registered outstanding loan loss provisions of 2.7% and write-offs of 0.5%. The weighted average yield has remained stable at 7% over the past years up to 2016.

MIV investments in MFIs affect millions of clients, of whom 70% are women and 55% live in rural areas. Over two-thirds of these MFI investees offer non-financial services, which is a sign of client centricity: enterprise development, adult education and literacy, health advice, agricultural extension and training, and women's empowerment. Almost all MIVs surveyed by Symbiotics also endorse the client protection principles of the Smart Campaign; in other words, there there is evidence that MIVs monitor how their investments affect the interaction of their investees with clients.

While these are rough signals showing that MIVs take into account the indirect effects of their investments, it leaves open the question of whether and how investments affect the double bottom line of a MFI, one way or another. To throw light on this question, it is useful to examine the nature of the financial instruments that pass through MIVs: 52 of the MIVs are fixed income funds, i.e. they exclusively provide debt. Nineteen MIV are mixed debt/equity and 22 are pure equity funds.[5] The nature of the investment instrument has a bearing on the extent to which investors can influence the social and financial orientation of a given MFI. Equity investors have a say on strategy decisions and the MFI's positioning in the local market facing competitors. Debt investors do not have the same degree of leverage but nevertheless can voice their concerns in renegotiations of the credit line – especially if the credit line is sizable.

Of the 22 pure equity MIVs, three had majority ownership on the board of the MFI, 10 had between 25% and 50% ownerships, and nine had less than 25% ownership. Half of these MIVs had a representative on the board. In five instances the representative of the MIV is also on the MFI's Social Performance Management Committee, which allows the investor to proactively monitor financial and social performance of the MFI.[6] The shareholder agreement that contractually binds MIV and MFI sometimes contains clauses related to social performance, for example compliance with "Client Protection Principles" (the case

Investing in microfinance 65

in 12 out of the 22 Equity Funds reviewed by Symbiotics). In some instances, the MIV explicitly commits the funded MFI to avoid mission drift. Every single one of the 22 equity MIVs report on social and environmental performance. So, as far as equity investments are concerned the MIV definitely has the means to make sure that mission drift does not occur – if it wants to.

Fixed income investments by MIVs are less intrusive. A typical covenant between an MIV and an MFI[7] can have wording that resonates very much like a mission statement:

> ...the purpose of the MFI shall be to provide ... accessible, transparent and competitive financial loans for micro, small, medium -sized enterprises and entrepreneurs... Particularly, the MFI shall have a social mission to alleviate poverty and to foster the creation of employment ... as an institution with a dual focus to generate commercial returns whilst remaining committed to a strong social mission.

Contractual commitments are the stick, but there are also carrots to nudge MFIs towards the kind of institutional performance that MIV investors want to see. Few MIVs offer preferential terms to financial institutions demonstrating a strong social performance commitment. Only 14 out of the 76 responding MIVs indicate that they offer or are planning to offer preferential terms (lower interest rates, technical assistance to improve social programmes, flexible tenors, flexibility on guarantees)[8] if the MFI improves on its social performance.

In some instances, MIV and the MFIs in its portfolio are so in tune that written obligations in covenants, shareholder agreements or incentives are not even needed. Both parties know exactly how much profitability and outreach to clients is good for the MFI and the MIV. Interests are particularly aligned, when MFIs of the same network decide to set up their own vehicle for equity investments. A case in point is the "WWB Microfinance Equity Fund."[9] In 2008 affiliates of Women's World Banking (WWB), a network of MFIs that finances small women entrepreneurs, set up a fund to make equity investments in MFIs primarily belonging to the network. The fund was intended to "protect and advance the WWB Network members mission of providing microfinance to low income women," while... "providing attractive returns."[10] Little risk of a clash on strategy here.

Even where MIVs and MFI are not from the same network, it is unlikely that MFIs are surprised by what is expected of them in terms of financial performance and social outreach: 76 MIVs (out of a total of

66 *Investing in microfinance*

85 responding) indicated that they expect a market rate of return and positive social returns. Only six give precedence to social returns and accept below market financial returns. Only two equity funds want to maximise financial returns (Figure 7.2)[11].

MIVs themselves have become the focus of interest with regard to their – indirect – social performance. In contrast to social performance measurement of individual MFIs for which standard norms have been developed and accepted,[12] it is much more complicated to measure the social performance of investors (MIVs) in terms of their influence on the double bottom line. In 2016, the University of Zürich's Centre for Microfinance presented a methodology to measure the social performance of Microfinance Investment Vehicles. It

> consists of a set of variables representing …the underlying MFIs… as well as indicators quantifying the mission of the MIV, its contribution to financial market development…, i.e. a set of nine efficient, comparable and measureable indicators at the level of the MIV with nine indicators at the MFI-level.[13]

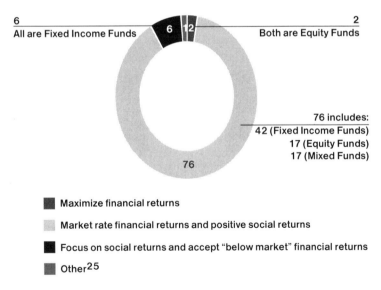

Figure 7.2 Return expectations of investors in microfinance.

Investing in microfinance 67

It is too early to say whether this methodology is being applied by MIVs. For the time being each MIV seems to prefer to work with its own performance measurement tools, which makes comparisons difficult. In an effort to align approaches, the European Microfinance Platform and the Social Performance Task Force therefore issued "Guidelines on Outcomes Management for Investors."[14] These Guidelines are to help and guide investors on how to monitor social outcomes attributable to the activities of the microfinance institutions that they invest in.

On balance, what are then the changes in the double bottom line that can be attributed to investments in MFIs? Several studies[15] suggest that the effect is mainly to reinforce the existing orientation of a MFI, but not to change it in the sense of mission drift. Given the wide range of microfinance investment vehicles, investors seem to select the fund vehicle that corresponds best to their own perception of double bottom line. They do not need to coerce the management of MFIs to become more commercial (or more poverty-focused): commercial investors ("finance first") select MIVs that have in their portfolios MFIs that already value superior financial performance, whilst development-oriented and social investors ("impact first") select MIVs that have portfolios of more socially minded MFIs. In the end, the goal mix of the investor is matched by the goal mix of the MFIs in the respective MIV portfolio. There does not appear to be much of mission drift in one direction or another – as a result of outside investments.

A word on "crowding-out": this is the charge that public development finance institutions (DFIs) like IFC, the regional development banks, KfW, FMO, Proparco, etc. distort the market of investments in microfinance, because they refuse to step aside for private investors once they have successfully demonstrated the business case. Instead DFIs – so it is claimed – hang around and continue to support large, established MFIs that do not need promotion any longer. Crowding-out is an issue in the relation between public and private investors, whether they are partners in the same MIV or promote separate vehicles. Crowding-out is neutral to mission drift – unless one would assimilate private investors to profit-maximisers. It is only when a clash erupts between public and private investors in the same MIV on the "right" way to steer and nudge MFIs in the portfolio. It is up to the fund managers like Blue Orchard, responsAbility, Symbiotics, etc. to arbitrate among their private and public investors when negotiating with MFIs, defining incentives, spelling out clauses in shareholder and debt agreements. Still: crowding-out and mission drift are two distinct issues. Crowding-out refers exclusively to expectations of financial performance, not social performance; and so far, nobody accused DFIs of crowding out social investors... (Figure 7.3).

68 *Investing in microfinance*

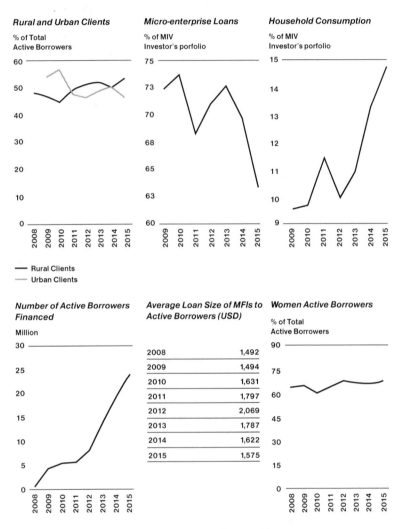

Figure 7.3 Social performance of MFIs with MIV investments.

Notes

1 This chapter focuses on the organised market for investments in microfinance. Obviously, there are also some investments taking place bilaterally outside of MIVs. There are for example crowdfunding platforms like KIVA that allow individuals to fund MFIs and their clients (www.kiva.org).
2 P. Goodman, *International Investment Funds – Mobilizing Investors towards Microfinance*, ADA Luxembourg, November 2003; Symbiotics/CGAP,

Investing in microfinance 69

Microfinance Funds 10 years, 2016; Microrate, The State of Microfinance Investment, 2011, R. Dominicé, Microfinance Investments, Symbiotics, 2012; see also CGAP Focus Notes on the subject; Symbiotics, 2017 MIV Survey – Market Data and Peer Group Analysis, September 2017.

3 Out of a total of 127 (http://symbioticsgroup.com/wp-content/uploads/2017/09/Symbiotics-2017-MIV-Survey.pdf). The figures in the following paragraphs are derived from this report.

4 Symbiotics (2017), op. cit., p. 36.

5 Symbiotics, 2017 MIV Survey – Market Data and Peer Group Analysis, September 2017, p. 29. Equity investors in microfinance have their own platform, the FIEC, a "membership council representing the leading private entities that make active, long term, and sustainable equity investments in institutions focusing on under- or un-served clients, with the goal of achieving greater financial inclusion" (https://fiecouncil.com/about-us/).

6 Symbiotics (2017), op. cit., p. 50.

7 This illustration has been provided by an anonymous MIV manager.

8 Symbiotics (2017) MIV Survey, p. 44.

9 Later baptided "Women's World Banking (WWB) Capital Partners."

10 Women's World Banking – Microfinance Equity Fund, New York, 2008.

11 Symbiotics (2017) Survey, op. cit., p. 46.

12 Like % of women served, average loan or deposit amount as % of per capita GNI, % of poor clients on total number of clients and so forth.

13 J. Meyer, A. Krauss, C. Nelung, *Measuring and Aggregating Social Performance of Microfinance Investment Vehicles*, Center for Microfinance, Department of Banking and Finance, University of Zürich, 2016, p. 34.

14 L. Spaggiari, Guidelines on outcomes management for investors, *European Dialogue*, No. 10, October 2016.

15 R. Mersland and L. Urgeghe, Performance and international investments in microfinance institutions in "International Debt Financing and Performance of Microfinance Institutions," *Strategic Change: Briefings in Entrepreneurial Finance*, vol. 22, no. 1–2, 2013, pp. 17–29; M. Moser, *Commercial Investments and Mission Drift in Microfinance: A Qualitative Analysis of Stakeholder Perceptions in Switzerland*, Haupt, 2013.

8 Subsidies

Donors are not all alike; some are hardly distinguishable from commercial investors in their insistence on rapid and full financial self-sufficiency, and some have a distinctly social agenda. The dividing line between investments and subsidies is not so clear. Practically all public investments contain elements of subsidies, for example credit lines provided at below market interest rates. These interest rebates range from 1% to 10% below the going market rate, so they can represent a substantial cost advantage to the MFI. Equity investments can also contain subsidy elements to the extent that they may voluntarily forego "normal" shareholder rights, like board representation or dividends.

Subsidies are hidden in public investments, but also come in the form of technical assistance, free staff training, provision of IT hardware, sponsoring of participation at conferences and other grants. In addition to these "retail" subsidies there are public investments into the financial infrastructure, like credit bureaus. These indirect subsidies are comparatively small as shares of global funding of microfinance, namely 4% (funding of infrastructure), 4% (clients like financial education, consumer protection, etc.), 2% (policymaking) and 7% (technical assistance).[1]

Not a single MFI would exist if it had not been for the well-meaning donor, government agency or international network that helped it at the start with some capital grant. Most MFIs continue to enjoy some form of ongoing subsidies. Clearly, with subsidies, donors and governments have instruments at their disposal that are possibly more powerful – and less volatile – than investments to nudge a MFI towards more profitability or – to the contrary – towards deeper outreach. Subsidies can alter the balance between financial and social goals in different ways, or – a third scenario – tolerate and reinforce the balance struck by the MFI's management between profit-orientation and social impact.

Subsidies 71

A 2016 study[2] found that practically all 1,335 MFIs with performance data on the MIX Market received some form of subsidy, from donors, governments, charities and socially responsible investors.[3] The total amount of subsidies awarded to these 1,335 MFIs in 2015 was $4.9 billion. According to Cull et al. (2009)[4] 61% of the total subsidies ($2.6 billion at that time) went to NGOs, i.e. the charter type of MFI most closely associated with deep outreach. 76% of the estimated $4.9 billion went to 932 MFIs that had been in business for more than 10 years, although in principle they should have reached full financial autonomy 10 years after their establishment[5] – at the latest.

Subsidies are considered legitimate and even necessary during the start-up phase until the MFI reaches maturity, scale and full control of its revenues and costs. In theory, subsidies are meant to help only in the initial years of a MFI's operation.[6] This is similar to the infant industry argument. With the completion of the running-in phase MFIs are expected to have attained full financial self-sufficiency. In fact, most MFIs – even those that count as mature, stable and self-financing – continue to receive subsidies. The targets of the 1990s may have been somewhat overambitious – or negligent of social performance.

Subsidies are intended as temporary support "to get an institution to the point where it can tap private funding sources, such as deposits."[7] The obsession with the sunset date has to be understood in the context of the early years of microfinance, when the claim of financial autonomy had to be vindicated. At that time, it seemed unusual that the distribution of small loans could be a serious business proposition. Performance of MFIs was then equated largely with financial performance of the institution doing the distribution. Obviously, news of the continued injection of subsidies – hidden and explicit – beyond the acceptable 10 years of the start-up phase would spoil the story. This perception changed over the years once it became clear that in order to maintain depth of outreach most MFIs needed some form of grant support. Subsidies began to irritate less. In fact, the stronger the recognition of the double bottom line in microfinance, the greater the acceptance of subsidies.

Subsidies are welcome and mostly well-intended, but they are not always healthy for the institution receiving them: they can send the wrong signals to management and induce slack performance. Programmes with subsidised, i.e. artificially lowered interest rates, often attract wrong, namely better-off clients with the appropriate connections, instead of the poor for whom they were intended. Subsidies from governmental sources undermine the MFI's independence. The appropriately

72 *Subsidies*

labelled "Subsidy Dependence Index (SDI)"[8] measures by how much "a lender would have to increase its revenue in order to cover costs if the lender had no access to subsidized resources." Receiving subsidies thus has a direct bearing on how the MFI prices its services and remains competitive.

Subsidies can also exacerbate the moral hazard problem in small loan transactions. If clients know that their loans come originally from a government subsidised credit line, then they tend to be less diligent to honour their repayment obligations towards the MFI. Not to speak of the direct market distorting effect on not-subsidised MFIs, which may be obliged to seek subsidies themselves or lower the interest rate further to the point of wiping out any residual profit. And then, subsidies are sticky, they seem to have a habit of staying on and are hard to phase out.[9]

Rather than becoming more efficient, microfinance markets appear to become more distorted, with a controversy about the roles of DFIs in developing microfinance markets and their practice of undercutting private investors. Development finance institutions (DFIs), like the World Bank, regional development banks, bilateral promotion banks like KfW, FMO and AFD, etc., continue to provide credit lines below the market rate. This may make sense in markets that need to be opened up, requiring a risk-taking pioneer like a DFI; it is counterproductive in markets that have developed and are ready to see the debt and equity investments by private actors. The last word on this phenomenon of "crowding-out" has not been spoken.[10]

Some of the arguments against subsidies in microfinance are not borne out empirically. Hudon and Tasca,[11] for example, find that subsidies are associated with a weaker financial performance, but that this is due to the depth of outreach and hence higher transaction costs per dollar delivered. Subsidies do not seem to lead to "rent-seeking" by staff and management of MFIs. The connection between subsidies and efficiency (= ratio of operating expense and loan portfolio) is less straightforward than assumed.[12] Not all subsidised MFIs are inefficient. ASA in Bangladesh, for example, is run efficiently in comparison with similar MFIs, although it is subsidised.[13] In fact, well-known MFIs that operate on a large scale and continue to have depth of outreach like Grameen Bank, SEWA, BRAC, Working Women's Forum, Pradhan, ASA, etc. still receive subsidies.[14] All of them have been in business for more than 10 years. On the other hand, there are MFIs that are profitable but less efficient than their competitors,

Subsidies 73

possibly because of (temporary) monopolistic market positions, as Table 8.1 suggests.

For individual MFIs, these subsidies can be substantial: Grameen Bank, for example, received about $175 million between 1985 and 1996, of which $16 million in direct grants, $81 million in saved capital costs due to concessional credit lines and $47 million in undistributed profits.[16] In 1996 the subsidies were the equivalent of 9% of the institution's portfolio.[17]

Most MFIs deal with several donors at the same time. This can be a bonanza as well as a nuisance. Having multiple donor partners on board gives a MFI tactical advantages to play one donor against the other. On the other hand, each donor insists on its own reporting format, and each donor may have its own special view on how the MFI should position itself in the space between profitability and social impact. In board meetings, this could lead to exciting debates on strategy. On the whole, though, just as investors pick a MIV that matches their strategy best, so do donors: they tend to select the sort of MFI that corresponds best to their own ideas of a balanced double bottom line. The variety and plurality of MIVs and MFIs protect the industry against mission drift through investments and subsidies.

While it may not make sense that financially self-sufficient MFIs continue to receive subsidies, there is at least one scenario that would justify it: if the MFI remains committed to depth of outreach and sustains, for example, a loss-making branch serving the very poor, i.e. if the social benefits its activities engender outweigh the costs to the taxpayer. A case in point is BRAC, a large MFI in Bangladesh, which initiated the IGVGD programme (Income Generation for Vulnerable Group Development). This programme targeted very

Table 8.1 Efficiency and profitability in Latin American MFIs[15]

MFIs (Latin America and Caribbean)	Efficiency (% operating expense ratio)	Profitability (% RoA)
Andes	13.0	1.8
FIE	10.0	3.1
WWBs	11.6–19.7	4.6–15.4
ADOPEM	17.0	11.7
Calpia	18.3	1.0
Compartamos	33.9	17.9
Confia	22.0	2.0
CMACs	12.5–17.7	3.1–7.1

74 *Subsidies*

poor women and made losses but was kept alive thanks to BRAC's other, more profitable programmes.[18] BancoSol in Bolivia, MiBanco in Peru, SKS in India and other large established MFIs similarly subsidise with internal resources specific programmes targeted at the very poor. "Cross-subsidisation" can be rewarded by external subsidies. More than rhetoric in mission statements, cross-subsidisation is evidence that the MFI acts in line with its vision and mission. Yet, for all these advantages cross-subsidisation presupposes that the MFI enjoys a domineering market position. Competition can reduce or even wipe out the margins that allow MFIs to cross-subsidise social programmes.

More generally, even "normal" and not so financially successful MFIs could need some sort of ongoing grant or subsidy element to ensure that they remain committed to the poorer segments of the population. In fact, these "normal" MFIs probably appreciate subsidies even more since they may not be able to cross-subsidise. This raises the question how subsidies can be used to make MFIs stick to their intended social performance – if the negative side effects of subsidies could be ruled out.

It can work with the right design. Like other public policy instruments subsidies can be designed in many different ways, having more or less distorting effects on market, institution and clients. Hence, the notion of "smart" subsidies[19] is defined as "carefully designed interventions that seek to minimize distortions, mis-targeting and inefficiencies while maximizing social benefits."[20] Certain types of subsidies are smart by themselves, because they do not discriminate between retail individual institutions but improve the general financial infrastructure, like sector-wide capacity building, technical assistance, refinancing and credit bureaus. Less smart are subsidies to individual microfinance institutions that affect costs and revenues like credit lines at below market rates, which undercut competition.

"Smart" subsidies are designed to be limited in time, decline and stop at a pre-negotiated exit date. They are performance-based. Benchmarks are set contractually, and non-compliance is sanctioned. Since microfinance institutions are – unlike banks – entities with a dual objective, performance is necessarily a composite of profitability and outreach. MFIs differ amongst themselves in the mix of these two objectives, so a fair measure of performance cannot be how profitable they are nor how far down they reach in poverty levels, but how *efficiently* the MFI combines profitability and outreach.[21]

Smart subsidies are still rare in practice. A major reason is that in order to be effective, they would need to be implemented in a

Subsidies 75

coordinated fashion – including the government. Attempts to bring together all actors in microfinance at the national level have been made, but these in-country coordination mechanisms never lasted very long.[22] In actual fact donors often chase attractive MFIs ("trophy lending")[23] and continue subsidising. Development banks, international NGOs, foundations and public bilateral agencies like to show their flag and be seen in association with success stories. Just as governments use microfinance programmes to buy votes.

Notes

1 CGAP Brief, Taking stock – recent trends in international funding for financial inclusion, December 2016, p. 2.
2 R. Cull, A. Demirguc-Kunt, and J. Morduch, The microfinance business model – enduring subsidy and modest profit, Policy Research Working Paper 7786, World Bank Development Research Group, August 2016.
3 Op. cit., p. 28.
4 R. Cull, et al., 2009, op. cit.
5 According to the 1995 Guidelines for the donor community intended to align their promotion of microfinance (the "Pink Book"), MFIs are expected to achieve "operational efficiency in three to seven years, and full self-sufficiency, i.e., covering all financing costs at non-subsidized rates within five to ten years...".
6 J. Morduch, Smart subsidy for sustainable microfinance, ADB Finance for the Poor, December 2005, vol. 6, no. 4.
7 CGAP, Building inclusive financial systems: donor guidelines on good practice in microfinance, Washington, 2004, p. 1.
8 J. Yaron, Assessing development financial institutions: a public interest analysis, World Bank Discussion Paper 174, Washington 1992.
9 J. Morduch, The role of subsidies in microfinance: evidence from the Grameen Bank, *Journal of Development Economics*, vol. 60, 1999.
10 D. von Stauffenberg and D. Rozas, Role Reversal revisited – are public development institutions still crowding out private investment in Microfinance, Microrate, 2011.
11 M. Hudon and D. Traca, Subsidies and Sustainability in Microfinance, ULB CEB Working Paper 06–20, October 2006.
12 The efficiency measures how many cents on average a MFI needs to deliver one dollar to the client.
13 J. Morduch, Smart ... op. cit., p. 3.
14 L. Bennett, et al., Ownership and sustainability – lessons on group-based financial services from South Asia, *Journal of International Development*, vol. 8, no. 2, 1996, pp. 271–288 and L. Webster, *The Informal Sector and Microfinance Institutions in West Africa*, World Bank, 1995.
15 Microrate and IADB, Performance Indicators for Microfinance Institutions – technical guide, July 2003, pp. 55 and 56.
16 J. Morduch, The role of subsidies in microfinance: evidence from the Grameen Bank, *Journal of Development Economics*, vol. 60, 1999, pp. 230–246.
17 Idem, p. 231.

76 Subsidies

18 J. Morduch, Smart subsidy ... op. cit., p. 5.
19 introduced to the microfinance field by Jonathan Morduch.
20 B. Armendariz and J. Morduch, *The Economics of Microfinance*, 2nd edition, MIT Press, 2010, p. 322.
21 B. Balkenhol, *Microfinance and Public Policy*, op. cit., p. 217.
22 D. Wright, In-Country Donor Coordination, CGAP Focus Note 19, April 2001.
23 Microrate, Role Reversal revisited, op. cit., p. 5.

9   Microfinance markets

Market size

According to the World Bank's Global Findex database[1] financial inclusion made significant progress over the past few years:

> the number of people worldwide having an account grew by 700 million between 2011 and 2014. 62 percent of the world's adult population has an account; up from 51 percent in 2011. Three years ago, 2.5 billion adults were unbanked. Today, 2 billion adults remain without an account.[2]

Still a large percentage of the population in many low-income countries remains without an account.[3] The gap between actual supply (i.e. loan portfolios or number of customers reached) and potential demand is signalled by the penetration rate. This is defined as the ratio of total borrowers served by MFIs to the size of a country's poor population living on less than $2 a day (MIX Market). By this measure financial inclusion thanks to microfinance is quite impressive in some countries (Table 9.1).

Millions of unbanked families constitute a "market" for microfinance institutions: individuals living on less than $2 a day or below the national poverty line. The job is therefore not yet done. Should it be the objective of the microfinance industry to reach all of them? Is that the upper limit of the market? Also, what about clients who simply do not want to interact with MFIs and rather deal with their habitual informal providers? Clearly, it would be misleading to equate "financially excluded" with "potential clients of microfinance institutions."

Moreover, the estimation of market size also depends on the definition of the penetration rate.[4] Most studies look only at clients as borrowers, not as depositors. This ignores the increasingly important

78 *Microfinance markets*

Table 9.1 Microfinance market penetration 2009

Country	MF Borrower accounts/active poor population
Bangladesh	25
Bosnia	15
Mongolia	15
Cambodia	13
Nicaragua	11
Sri Lanka	10
Montenegro	10
Vietnam	10
Peru	10
Armenia	9
Bolivia	9
Thailand	8
India	7

use of savings services, insurance, payment and other offerings. Even if one considers the billions of unbanked individuals worldwide as a potential market for microfinance it may well be that with the existing business models microfinance is unable to reach them. The approximately 200 million current microfinance clients may represent the "low-hanging fruit." This recognition has prompted recent studies[5] of financial inclusion to shift the focus from counting sheer client numbers to the promotion of "market development" and "market systems," i.e. a comprehensive approach to financial inclusion.

This chapter examines the interactions among financial service providers when markets become competitive. In particular, we explore whether and how these interactions influence the double bottom line of MFIs, in terms of financial results and outreach.

Concentration

Markets allow buyers and sellers to exchange goods and services. In the exchange process they establish a price. This also applies to microfinance: there are several thousands of specialised microfinance institutions offering their services, and there are tens of millions of household-enterprises and individuals contracting loans and making deposits. However, market configurations in real life show that the conditions for a near-perfect, efficient market (i.e. a multitude of buyers

Table 9.2 Market concentration (active borrower accounts Bangladesh 2009)[9]

MFI	Borrowers ('000)	%	Gross loan portfolio (Tk '000)	%
Grameen Bank	6,426	23.8	54,715	28.9
BRAC	6,241	23.1	43,879	23.2
ASA	4,000	14.8	31,322	16.5
Proshika	1,706	6.3	3,747	2.0
Buro	621	2.3	4,051	2.1
TMSS	504	1.9	3,613	1.9
Swanirvar	452	1.7	1,828	1.0
RDRS	285	1.1	1,140	0.6

and sellers, informed market actors that respond to price changes and comparable products and services) are not the rule.

In reality, there is considerable concentration in some microfinance markets. In Uganda, Bangladesh and Bolivia, for example, the respectively four largest MFIs control over 50%, 69% and 71% of the total national microloan portfolios.[6] It is true that market concentration does not necessarily translate into lack of competition: in Bangladesh "a typical middle-size village will have a branch of Grameen, BRAC, ASA, three or four middle-size NGO-MFIs and three or four local ones."[7] This would suggest that despite overall concentration in terms of loan assets and client numbers[8] no single MFI in Bangladesh enjoys a position of monopoly. Yet, confronted with over 550 licensed NGO-MFIs and an almost equal number of unlicensed NGOs, the three largest microfinance organisations (Grameen, BRAC, ASA), which catered in 2011 to approximately 62% of all microfinance borrower accounts and close to 70% of overall outstanding loans, have the clout to influence the development of the market, in particular interest rates and the terms at which MFIs are refinanced and subsidised (Table 9.2).

Competition

Competition is, in principle, good for clients of microfinance institutions, because it forces MFIs to become more efficient, innovative and client-centred. Market price, i.e. the interest rate, is a major indicator of the efficiency in financial intermediation and should be easy to determine. However, many MFIs have the habit of hiding costs in the effective interest rate and not telling the client. A comparison of interest rates between MFIs can be misleading because some MFIs factor in

80 *Microfinance markets*

upfront fees, while others do not; some MFI calculate the interest rate on a declining basis, while others use a flat basis and occasionally the client may be obliged to make a security deposit. Prices of microloans are not always exactly transparent.[10]

Still, the big picture shows that – while the interest rates on microloans are still high – there is a decline[11] over a seven-year period. over time and with the entrance of more and more microfinance service providers onto the market – including banks – interest rates tend to go down. That seems to be borne out by the following graph (Figure 9.1)[12].

A second perspective on the microfinance market is to look at the differentials with prices charged by comparable service providers, whether formal (banks), semiformal (cooperatives) and informal (moneylenders). The graph that follows suggests that in Bolivia, a market characterised by competition between and among different types of financial institutions, interest rates charged by microfinance institutions – while remaining high in comparison – progressively approach the rates of other financial institutions over a period of 15 years (Figure 9.2)[13].

The declining interest rates in microfinance may be good news for borrowers, but microfinance practitioners are less enthusiastic. In response to the "Banana Skin Survey"[14] several hundred leading microfinance practitioners identified competition as the number one challenge in 2008 and ranked it in 3rd place in 2011 and 2014. It is still widely seen as the main reason for overselling of credit and client over-indebtedness.

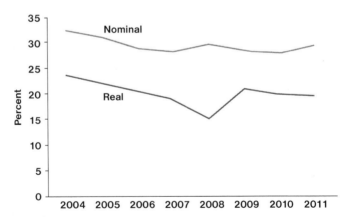

Note: Global interest and fee income from loans/average total GLP, weighted by GLP, both nominal and net of inflation.

Figure 9.1 Global Interest Yield Trends in microfinance 2004–2011.

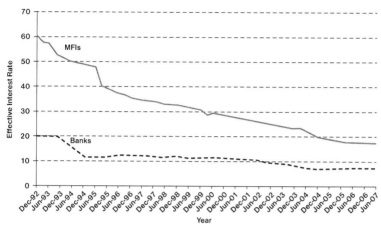

Figure 9.2 Evolution of interest rates of banks and MFIs (Bolivia 1992–2007).

To understand the uneasiness of microfinance managers about competition, one needs to look at the composition of the gross margin generated by a microfinance institution (Figure 9.3)[15].

In response to competition and subsequent pressures on the interest rate, a microfinance institution can compress one or several of the four components that make up the gross yield: operating costs, financing costs, provisions for loan losses and net profit. Three of these four cost components are hard to cut *in the short-run*: financing costs are hardest to bring down in the short-run as MFIs are tied by contractual obligations in multi-year credit lines that cannot be quickly adjusted. The provisions for loan losses cannot simply be compressed: a prudent manager is well advised to be prepared for eventual rising default rates and late repayments in an increasingly competitive environment. To lower operating expenses, MFIs can boost productivity, close branches, lay off staff, introduce an incentive-based salary system,[16] discontinue non-financial services or combine all of these. Again, the effects do not materialize overnight. What remains as a component of the gross yield that can be compressed in the short-run is the residual, net profit. In practice it is the net profit that tends to be curtailed in the short-run when the MFI confronts competition.

All of the aforementioned responses to competition presuppose that the MFI remains focused on its current clientele. However, a more convenient and radical alternative is to replace the many very small – and

82 Microfinance markets

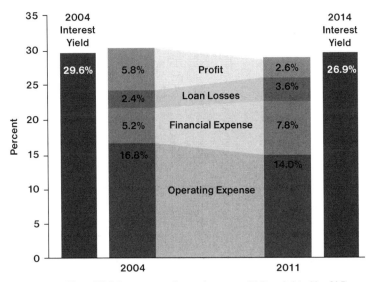

Figure 9.3 Components of interest yields in microfinance 2004–2011.

costly – transactions by a few larger loans. This would mean "mission drift." Competition could, in this scenario, severely affect the double bottom line.

Competitive pressures are further aggravated by the entry of commercial banks into the microfinance market. It is true that many very small, costly transactions with opaque clients is not exactly what a commercial bank would see as its prime market segment, but compared to microfinance institutions coming out of the NGO mould they have a number of advantages: a brand name, infrastructure, a full range of services allowing them to cross-subsidise, access to capital and above all a regulated status.

Market saturation

The most obvious response to competition for an individual MFI is to grow and expand its loan portfolio. If, however, several MFIs take the same decision at the same time, then the entire national market gets quickly saturated. "The rapid growth in lending capacity created by abundant funding and new entrants for whom microfinance is a product

Microfinance markets 83

rather than a mission."[17] Market saturation is defined as the threshold reached by a significant degree of market penetration, expressed as the number of individual borrowers per adult population. The upper limit is determined by the number of clients (borrowers) that "the market can be expected to sustainably support."[18] Market saturation manifests itself via different symptoms: within a relatively short time, households enter obligations towards several microfinance institutions (multiple loans). Another sign is client poaching, i.e. MFIs seek to lure away clients from other MFIs. As a result, clients may end up having more loans and debt obligations than they can handle, obliging them to take up expensive informal loans to honour debt obligations to MFIs (debt recycling).

Rapid portfolio growth does by itself not automatically lead to a deterioration of portfolio quality,[19] but if the loan portfolios of individual microfinance institutions grow in a market that already has a significant level of microfinance market penetration, then these loan portfolios tend to turn sour, i.e. clients do not or cannot honor their repayment obligations. Based on 3,263 observations from 821 MFIs in 91 countries reporting data for 2000–2008, Gonzalez finds that "high levels of penetration rates (over 10 percent of total population) and high aggregate country growth levels in number of microfinance borrowers (over 63 percent per year), is … associated with a deterioration of portfolio quality."[20] Rapid portfolio growth can lead to over-indebtedness and a deterioration of the portfolio. In other words, both clients and MFIs are worse off in a scenario of uncontrolled multiple lending. To contain these risks the association of Indian microfinance operators (MFIN) took the initiative to promote credit bureaus and voluntary codes of conduct, like the self-imposed limitation to three loans and a maximum combined amount of Rs 50,000 ($1,000) per client.[21]

Competition and mission drift

Mission drift shows by a substantial increase of average loan amounts expressed as GDP per head. The following table signals how this ratio evolved over a 16-year period for MFIs operating in Latin America. MFIs pursue different performance paths, with some retaining the focus on a given poverty level of their clientele, while others move slowly up into larger transactions,[22] and yet others show no clear direction one way or the other. Obviously, mission drift cannot be attributed only to competition; it can also be the result of a deliberate strategic decision to reposition the MFI (Table 9.3).

Most MFIs prefer to remain loyal to their double bottom line. Rather than fundamentally change their business model, they rather innovate

84 *Microfinance markets*

Table 9.3 Mission drift? Average loan amounts/GDP per head (%) of selected Latin American MFIs 1990–2006

MIX Market data	1990	1999	2006
FIE	91	99	128
Mibanco	11	13	49
Banco Estado	9	21	37
PRODEM	21	51	157
Bancosol	21	92	142
ADEMI	17	121	81

in the design of products and services, for example by phasing out group loans and replacing them by individual loans, or by extending the maturity of microloans. The promise of progressively larger loans to the same entrepreneurial poor is also an option that helps to control costs and create customer loyalty ("graduation approach"). The MFI may also decide to be more flexible in its requirements for collateral. Better customer service (quicker turnarounds, mobile banking, agent banking with retail shops and more meaningfully scheduled interactions enhancing the convenience for clients) are also options that can help a MFI to position itself more effectively in the market, without resorting to dramatic cuts in services. Lastly, a MFI that is reluctant to undergo these tedious internal improvements can – provided it has the required means – buy another MFI. Mergers and acquisitions between microfinance institutions are a way to cope with competition whilst pursuing a growth path and keeping the original double bottom line.[23]

The empirical evidence concerning the effects of competition on the double bottom line of MFIs is mixed. Competition does not generally seem to lead to mission drift. Reviewing the MIX Market data for 342 MFIs, Cull et al. (2009)[24] find that

> greater competition, as indicated by greater bank penetration in the overall economy, is associated with deeper outreach by the microfinance institutions, suggesting that competition pushes micro-banks toward poorer markets, as reflected by smaller average loans sizes and greater outreach to women.

Also based on MIX Market data on over 500 MFIs in the period from 2003 to 2010 A.K. Kar and R.B. Swain arrive at the conclusion that "increased competition in the microfinance sector leads to improved depth of outreach and profitability of the sampled MFIs. The data also supports the view that increased competition increases loan portfolio quality."[25] Their findings suggest that "competition among MFIs is actually not bad as it improves their performance (social and financial) and loan portfolio quality."[26] What seems to make a difference is the fact that the MFIs themselves anticipate client over-indebtedness and agree to set up a system to share client information.

No matter which options the MFI chooses to cope with competition and whatever component of the gross yield it compresses, the net yield, i.e. its profit, is likely to shrink gradually. MFIs are no longer as profitable now as they used to be in the 1990s and 2000s, and this is largely due to increasing competition amongst MFI – and the entry of banks and other financial institutions into this market.

As long as MFIs emphasise the two sides of the double bottom line differently, competition is likely to force cost-cutting on all market participants, and those with a more social agenda (reflected in client proximity, a broad range of services and products other than credit, presence in remote rural areas) may find themselves in a situation where they have to rebalance their performance goals. This dilemma has been recognised in the donor community, which seems to be prepared to support the double bottom line and outreach to the poor of MFIs that, risk mission drift as a result of competition.

Notes

1 www.worldbank.org/en/programs/globalfindex.
2 Idem.
3 See the World Bank's FINDEX index.
4 For a discussion of the concept "penetration rate" in the literature, see Krauss, et al., op. cit., p. 5.
5 CGAP Focus Note 105, Development Finance Institutions and Financial Inclusion: From Institution-Building to Market Development, March 2017.
6 CGAP, Competition and Microcredit Interest rates, Focus Note 33, February 2006, op. cit. p. 10.
7 Quoting S. Rutherford, in: D. Pine, *The Microfinance Sector in Bangladesh: Innovation or Stagnation*, BA Thesis in Banking and Finance, Center for Microfinance, University of Zürich, 2010, p. 39.
8 See following table from S. Sinha, *Bangladesh Microfinance Review*, 2011, p. 4.
9 S. Sinha, *Bangladesh Microfinance Review*, 2011, p. IV.
10 C. Waterfield, *Transparency in Microfinance – The Client Perspective*, UMM/ Frankfurt School, Frankfurt July 2012 (www.mftransparency.org).
11 CGAP, Microcredit interest rates and their determinants, Access to Finance Forum, June 2013, p. 6.
12 Are Microcredit Interest Rates Excessive? CGAP Brief, February 2009, p. 2: "the decline by 2.3 percentage points a year between 2003 and 2006... was ...much faster than bank rates".

86 *Microfinance markets*

13 CGAP, The New Moneylenders: Are the Poor Being Exploited by High Microcredit Interest Rates? Occasional Papers 15, February 2009, p. 8.
14 www.csfi.org/financial-inclusion-banana-skins.
15 R. Rosenberg, et al., Microcredit interest rates and their Determinants 2004–2011, CGAP, June 2013, p. 21.
16 Notably by raising productivity (see ABA's incentive scheme in Egypt).
17 Microfinance Banana Skins 2014 – Facing Reality, p. 7.
18 E. Javoy and D. Rozas, MIMOSA 2.0: Mapping the (micro)credit cycle, 2015.
19 A. Gonzalez, op. cit., p. 1: "the sheer pace of growth does little by itself to explain portfolio quality problems."
20 A. Gonzalez, Is microfinance growing too fast? *MIX Data Brief No. 5*, June 2010.
21 D. Rozas and S. Sinha, Avoiding a microfinance bubble in India: is self-regulation the answer? *Microfinance Focus*, 10 January 2010.
22 Whether accompanying their existing stock of clients or by substituting poorer clients by less poor clients.
23 In 2014, Grupo ACP sold 60% of its shares in MiBanco to Financiera Edyficar, Peru's second-largest microfinance institution, owned by Creditcorp, the largest holding company of the country. After the merger about 900,000 clients would be reached by the new entity and close to 20% of the microfinance market. (MICROCAPITAL BRIEF 21.2.2014: "Creditcorp's Financiera Edyficar of Peru to Acquire 61% Stake in Mibanco for $179m"; www.microcapital.org).
24 R. Cull, A. Demirgüc-Kunt and J. Morduch, *Microfinance Trade-Offs: Regulation, Competition and Financing*, 2009, op. cit., p. 154.
25 A.K. Kar and R.B. Swain, *Competition, performance and portfolio quality in microfinance markets – a study using global panel data*, University of Helsinki, 2014. The authors emphasise, though, that their set of MFIs has a disproportionately large share of established commercially oriented institutions in Latin America. Also, in their calculations of profitability, they did not take into account subsidies, grants and donations, which may overstate the RoA indicator.
26 A.K. Kar and R.B. Swain, op. cit., p. 18.

10 Public policy

Imagine a microfinance institution in a remote rural part of a country. It caters to several thousand poor clients, most of them women. The poverty of clients shows in the very small size of average loans (3.1% of GNI per head) and very small deposits. This microfinance institution is the only financial service provider locally. It has a strong social commitment and offers a range of non-financial services. Compared to benchmarks in its peer group, the MFI is efficient, but it would be obliged to close down if it was not for grants from private donors and subsidies by aid agencies and the government.

From a strict financial angle, a continuation of subsidies could not really be justified, as this MFI would not reach financial autonomy for a long time to come; but microfinance institutions are not purely commercial actors. Policymakers also have to consider the social costs and consequences of a reduction or withdrawal of subsidies. A substantial number of poor households would be deprived of the access to the only financial service provider available locally. Given the stagnant economic conditions in this remote part of the country it is unlikely that a bank or another service provider would take its place. It is even conceivable that the government would be forced to open its own mechanism for the distribution of allowances and payments, obviously at considerable costs to the taxpayer.

This case illustrates the challenges of public policy in microfinance: any decision must take into account a host of factors bearing on consumers, institutions, markets, principles of policy and hard-nosed electoral politics. The consensus in the microfinance industry in the 1990s was that microfinance institutions would, in the end, become financially self-sufficient – some sooner, others later – and that public policy was therefore not really needed.

This changed from the 2000s on mainly for two reasons. The discovery of the multitude of business models in microfinance, and second,

88 *Public policy*

a growing awareness that the more socially oriented MFIs would require longer-term outside support to keep their poverty focus. Several arguments have been put forward to justify some form of government intervention in the microfinance market:

1 Access to finance is an entitlement,[1] an idea advanced by M. Yunus.[2] Only because an individual is poor should not be a reason to exclude her from essential financial transactions. If the market does not provide equal opportunities for all, then the state has to rectify this market failure.
2 Most low-income countries have no comprehensive social security systems; in such conditions the access of poor households to affordable and suitable financial instruments is vital to allow them to protect themselves against shocks, accidents and misfortune. In this view, public policy should encourage MFIs to innovate in savings, insurance and other risk-mitigation products.
3 Financial inclusion is a necessary condition for incomes and jobs in small and microenterprises. They make up the vast majority of all firms with most jobs. Governments committed to broad-based growth have an interest in promoting financial intermediaries capable of catering to small and microenterprises that often tend to be excluded.
4 Access to finance is key for the attainment of several Sustainable Development Goals (SDGs). Overcoming access barriers would be an efficient way to use scarce fiscal resources for a host of essential public goods: education, housing, clean air and water, renewable energy, transport, etc.
5 Exclusion from financial markets and discriminatory practices by financial service providers can reinforce a feeling amongst millions of being left behind. For stability, social and economic, it is therefore preferable to have a broad based, accessible and diverse financial sector. Public policy can steer the market towards that configuration.
6 As the global financial crisis demonstrated, a diversified financial sector happens to be more resilient against systemic shocks. That means that the ideal institutional landscape should have a place for agents that are more socially oriented, private or public or mixed and operate in a comprehensive financial infrastructure with credit-rating facilities, guarantee funds and so forth. Smart public policy interventions in time make subsequent ad hoc expensive rescue operations redundant.

Public policy in theory

Efficiency

Considering that microfinance was initially meant to take off without any outside support as a self-sustaining, market-based strategy, the reference to public policy is somewhat surprising. Microfinance would need no promotion, as it would fly by its own means. And yet a host of aid programmes continue to foster financial institutions, infrastructure and markets for more inclusion at an estimated cost of $31 billion.[3] So clearly there is some public policy happening. As in other domains, governments can do benefit and harm by their interventions. So, it may be helpful to recall two rules that should guide public policy in general.

The first rule is that any intervention of public policy should not cost more than the expected benefits, whether for the clients, microfinance institutions and the entire market. To illustrate this point with the MFI in South Africa presented at the beginning of this chapter: the total outlay in cash transfers, training, equipment and credit lines for the MFI should be outweighed by the expected income and welfare gains made by the clients, the revenue situation of the MFI and budgetary savings on welfare payments. This rule-of-thumb calculation makes sense intuitively; however, in real life, policy decisions are rarely made on the basis of a prior cost benefit analysis. Instead they are based on implicit and approximate assumptions about the number of poor people reached, the likelihood that no other financial service provider would replace the MFI, should it disappear, and the budgetary implications of large numbers of rural poor all of a sudden needing welfare transfers: assumptions that are subjective and biased.

The second rule – more specific to the field of microfinance – is that a public policy intervention should respect the business models of the institutions and not change their mission – deliberately or inadvertently. As we have seen in Chapter 6, there is a range of approaches in microfinance, from very commercial at one end to very social at the other. A public intervention that would – deliberately or unintentionally – alter the missions of the MFIs would no longer be neutral and alter the entire institutional landscape. Clients would no longer have the same choice between different types of MFIs. Apart from that, it is questionable whether it is up to government agencies to make MFIs more commercial – or more social. Isn't it the role of public policy to induce MFIs to do better – i.e. to become

90   *Public policy*

more efficient – regardless of the business model: NGOs, financial cooperatives, microfinance banks and so forth?

Variety of institutional models in microfinance is presumably better for society as it covers a broader range of financial needs. Variety makes the market more dynamic, resilient and open to innovations. Outreach to the poor is not likely to improve if in response to government policy all MFIs turned into profit-maximisers. Again, this rule of neutrality and respect for the plurality of business models in microfinance looks self-evident and plausible, but governments and aid agencies rarely look at the microfinance market as a whole with its diversity of MFIs but prefer to support individual institutions with which they are familiar and that happen to have the largest client numbers or the most convincing communication strategy.

Instruments of public policy

Broadly, one can distinguish three sets of measures of public policy: capacity building, regulation and funding. Capacity building, i.e. the transfer of competencies to enhance decision-making by MFIs, makes up 7% of all public policy resources going into microfinance.[4] Capacity building on the client side, i.e. financial literacy and improved management of grass roots organisations, amounts to roughly 4%. Second, regulation, i.e. the formulation and enforcement of norms governing the operations of financial institutions and the functioning of the financial market as a whole stands at about 4% of the total funding for microfinance. The third type of public policy measures is the injection – or withdrawal – of financial resources to institutions, for example through credit lines at preferential rates. This is the predominant instrument of public policy. Funding as debt or equity can go to MFIs directly or via national funds or apexes. Overall funding (debt, equity, grants) of microfinance and financial inclusion stood at $34 billion with 70% of this from public sources. In other words, in one year public policy agents (DFIs, multilateral and bilateral agencies) channelled $23.8 billion to microfinance and financial inclusion. This is more than what donor agencies and multilaterals allocated to agriculture and rural development: $14 billion (2013).[5]

1. Capacity building

Financial exclusion is less the consequence of a lack of money than of a lack of trust, which itself is the result of insufficient information. In most low-income economies, banks have excess liquidities, while

Public policy 91

at the same time millions of households and enterprises in the same economies struggle to enter and maintain stable relations with a formal financial institution. Chapter 2 argued that it is primarily this lack of information about the effective risks of loan default that gave rise to microfinance. Public policy seeks to raise the level of transparency in the financial market by enhancing the capacities of all agents to interact smartly and responsibly: at the micro level, it is the capacity of retail institutions and their clients; at the intermediary level, it is the capacity of the agencies that make up the market infrastructure and that facilitate financial contracts; and at the macro level, it is the capacity of the central bank, bank regulators and other regulatory and supervisory agencies.

The capability of clients to enter into financial contracts shows in their "financial education."[6] Consumer awareness and financial literacy deserve to be promoted by governments because they "contribute to market development and ... financial stability."[7] Financial capability or literacy embraces financial *knowledge* (for example how to calculate the effect of the interest rate on the balance in a deposit account, or how to figure out the effective cost of a loan with fees of x and annual interest of z)[8], as well as financial *attitude* that probes into respondents' liquidity preferences, their inclination to track spending and earnings, to stick to financial commitments and their anticipation of the costs of basic expenses such as food and clothes.

Financial education can enhance financial literacy, i.e. a better grasp of the key notions in finance and thus a better understanding of the costs and risks of a financial contract; but whether financial education also has a robust impact on the actual behaviour of individuals is still being discussed.[9]

Capacity building on the supply side of finance addresses this deficit via training of staff of MFIs.[10] It focuses on techniques to find out which products and services the clients really want and can afford, and how to develop these products. Some household-enterprises grow more rapidly than others, while some diversify after a period of growth and others concentrate on one single income-generating activity and specialise in it. Some clients take to insurance as a means of mitigating risks, while others find the entire concept of insurance unappealing. A smart loan officer knows his clients' preferences and acts accordingly.

Capacity building of decision makers in agencies responsible for the infrastructure of the financial market[11] deals with the challenges in regulating and supervising financial institutions with a high share of uncollateralised loans. Should – and if so, under which conditions – financial intermediaries be allowed to take substitutes for conventional

92 *Public policy*

collateral? How can local banks be motivated to refinance local MFIs? What is the safest way to anticipate the likelihood of a systemic crisis following massive loan defaults in one or several microfinance institutions? Can regulation be delegated to the microfinance institutions themselves without running systemic risks?

Overall capacity building (training courses, seminars, webinars and other measures) at the various levels are estimated to cost donors and governments some 4% of the total funding flow[12] of $23.8 billion, i.e. over $900 million per annum.

2. Norms and rules[13]: regulating the environment and operations

WHY REGULATE MFIS?[14]

In many parts of the world, microfinance started significantly to take off when NGOs realised that they could make their services more attractive by adding microfinance to community development, group formation, literacy training, sensitisation about health issues and so forth. These NGOs were set up to do general development work, not finance. As long as the money for these new activities came from abroad and private sources, this was not problematic. All that was needed was to register and report on where the money came from and where it went and at what rates, just to be transparent.

Matters got complicated when public money (domestic or international) began to move in to the field of microfinance – even more so if a MFI started to accept deposits, even in small amounts and on a limited scale, and get into the business of financial intermediation. What would happen to small depositors if the MFI became insolvent? Donor agencies and international networks can look after themselves, but the small depositor needs the protecting hand of the state. Imposing a minimum of prudential regulation has motivated governments to protect the public, in particular small depositors.

Another rationale for regulating and supervising the microfinance sector is the (perceived) inherent volatility and greater exposure to risk. After all, many MFIs lend to customers without taking tangible collateral. So, if central banks have good reasons to impose rules and norms on banks, there would seem to be an even stronger case for regulating microfinance institutions. Actually, the evidence shows that loan default rates in microfinance are consistently inferior to bank default rates.

Public policy 93

A third rationale for regulation and supervision of MFIs is that they cannot mobilise shareholders' capital as quickly as banks so as to respond to a temporary crisis in liquidity, solvency or capital structure. The governance in NGO-type MFIs is not exactly clear: who owns it actually? The donor agencies that made some grants for the start-up capital? The representatives of international NGOs networks that sit on the board of the MFI but have no real financial stake? The managers running the MFI?

WHAT IS TO BE REGULATED?[15]

In 2010, the Bank for International Settlement in Basel defined 25 principles for deposit-taking MFIs.[16] These are adapted from the corresponding set of rules for banks to the specific requirements of microfinance covering governance and ownership, capital adequacy, risk management, provisions and reserves, market risks and interest rate risks and so forth.

Such an all-encompassing approach to MFI regulation and supervision can push supervisory agencies in low-income countries to the limit. Clearly, regulation and supervision entail costs, and these need to be weighed against the expected benefits. In actual practice, regulation and supervision encompass core obligations to register, to disclose ownership, to make financial statements public and to submit periodic reports and more strictly "prudential" regulation that "aims to reduce the risk that depository institutions will fail."[17]

The following seven features warrant particular attention in microfinance:

> *minimum capital requirements*: Given the overall smaller volume of microfinance activities, the minimum capital requirements are also smaller in absolute terms. The Bank of Uganda regulation, for example, sets the requirement for deposit taking MFI at 1/50 of the corresponding rule for banks,[18] in Ghana it is at 1/60.[19] One can also relate the minimum capital requirements to per capita GDP, which presupposes a nexus of this regulatory aspect to a country's economic and financial sector development.[20] More significant is the ratio of capital to assets taking into account the portfolio risk. In some countries regulators are more rigorous with MFIs than with banks: in India banks have to hold a minimum capital of 9% of risk-weighted assets, while MFIs are required to have a ratio of 15%.[21]
>
> *capital adequacy*: in the UEMOA zone in West Africa the PARMEC law[22] stipulates that the loan portfolio of member-owned

94 *Public policy*

MFIs must not exceed the double of deposits. In comparison to the leverage allowed in banking this rule looks conservative, but it is motivated by scepticism whether MFIs are able to manage portfolio risk. Other considerations that tend towards stricter capital adequacy rules in microfinance institutions than in banks are the limited diversification in the loan portfolios in MFIs, market saturation coupled with client over-indebtedness and the large proportion of unsecured loans.[23]

asset quality: MFI are obliged to track and document late repayments by clients and loan delinquencies and to record these based on generally accepted accounting rules for provisioning and write-offs: outstanding principal balance of all loans past due more than x days/ outstanding principal balance of all loans (portfolio at risk, PAR).[24]

risk concentration: the PARMEC law, for example, stipulates that no single client can have more than 10% of the total loan portfolio. Apart from that a MFI is not constrained by regulation for how it diversifies its loan portfolios between different sectors, regions and client categories.

insider lending: generally, this should not be an issue in microfinance institutions. Their business is to lend to the poor, so it is hardly imaginable that a manager or board member is tempted to borrow from the MFI. Cooperatively organized MFIs may be an exception as their management is entrusted to members on a voluntary basis. If a member has a borrower status at the time of assuming a management function, it would not seem realistic to expect that the loan be put hold. The PARMEC law in the West therefore does not prohibit insider lending in principle: it just stipulates that managers cannot hold more than 20% of the total portfolio.

reserves and liquidity: according to the PARMEC law 15% of net profit must be ploughed back into the reserves. A specific liquidity risk in microfinance is the uncertainty of donor funding. While this cannot be directly regulated, MFIs can be required to report the source, terms and duration of donor funding.

ownership: concentration of ownership of a MFI is not necessarily an issue to merit regulation, but the transfer of ownership is. Principle 4 of the Basel Committee Core Principles deals with the issue of a transfer of significant part of ownership. It observes that the "supervisor has the power to review and reject any proposals to transfer significant ownership or controlling interests held directly or indirectly in existing banks to other parties." The Basel Committee reckons that MFIs are to be treated exactly like banks in this respect.[25]

Public policy 95

EFFECTS OF REGULATION

What does regulation do to a microfinance institution, in particular to its double bottom line? Studies undertaken so far find that "microfinance institutions subjected to more rigorous and regular supervision are as profitable as others, despite facing higher costs of supervision."[26] In particular, MFIs that transform so as to be authorised to collect deposits discovered that deposits are indeed a cheaper and/or more stable source of capital. On the other hand, regulation and supervision also seem to be associated with a slight form of mission drift: "larger average loan sizes...and less lending to women."[27]

If the regulatory framework is tailored to the type of MFI that happens to be predominant in the country (NGOs in the case of the MENA region or financial cooperatives in West and Central Africa), then regulation may inadvertently prevent the emergence of other forms of MFIs.[28]

CLIENT PROTECTION

No amount of regulation of financial service providers can alter the fundamental fact that banks and other financial institutions have more clout and leverage than their clients. Policymakers have therefore sought to complement regulation with appeals for voluntary self-restraint and code of conduct. In the aftermath of diverse microfinance crises in Bosnia, Morocco, Nicaragua and India, representatives of several international support networks called in 2008 for a voluntary code of conduct ("Pocantino Declaration")[29] to ensure "that providers of financial services to low-income populations take concrete steps to protect their clients from potentially harmful financial products and ensure that they are treated fairly." The key points were subsequently synthesised into "Client Protection Principles." A broad coalition of MFIs and international networks, "The Smart Campaign," was launched to promote knowledge of and adherence to these principles worldwide.

The Client Protection Principles[30] are not part of regulation and supervision strictly speaking, as no MFI will be penalised if it refuses to subscribe to them. Still, they are part of the system of norms that should guide the interaction between poor clients and financial institutions. Codes of conduct in the financial sector may serve the industry's good name, but objectively they also reinforce a sense of fairness and equity, which are goals of public policy. The absence of legal enforcement does not make them less effective: with more and more MFIs endorsing the Client Protection Principles – currently close to

96   Public policy

1,700[31] – and with the pressure built up in donor agencies and international support networks, any MFI that is concerned about its good name is well advised to avoid doing anything that might come close to violating these principles.

The Client Protection Principles deal with six aspects of the loan cycle:

- Avoidance of over-indebtedness: credit only if demonstrated ability of the client to repay.
- Pricing, terms and conditions of financial products need to be transparent and understandable to clients.
- Collection of loans due should be civilised.
- Staff should treat microfinance clients correctly.
- There should be a mechanism in place to settle complaints by clients.
- Privacy of Client Data must be safeguarded.

INTEREST RATE POLICY

Public policy influences the prices of microfinance. MFIs are subjected to monetary policy[32] like all other financial institutions. One particular monetary policy tool that stands out as controversial is the imposition of **interest rate ceilings**.[33] Seventy-six countries have such price controls, most of them in sub-Sahara Africa and Latin America.[34] The cap is set in relation to the effective interest rate or the annual percentage rate. The cap – or rather caps, as most price control regimes provide for a range of ceilings for different credit products – can be expressed in absolute terms (as the 24% cap in the West African Economic and Monetary Union [WAEMU] in West Africa) or in relation to a benchmark rate in the financial market.[35]

The rationale for interest rate ceilings is the concern to protect clients from the risks of over-indebtedness, abuse by predatory lenders and new barriers to finance. The poor are said to need to be protected against financial institutions charging exorbitant interest rates. The high level of microfinance interest rates suggests huge underlying profit margins. This is, however, not the case as the preceding chapters have shown. The high interest rate is mainly a function of costs. A study of 456 MFIs shows an average gross yield of 26.9%. This was made up mostly of operating costs (14%), capital costs (7.8%) and loan losses (3.6%). Only 2.6%, i.e. less than 10% of the interest rate charged, was for gross profit of the MFI.[36] In an extreme case, a cap can wipe out the entire profit margin and oblige the MFI to adjust its business model.

Public policy 97

Despite the criticism, governments continue to resort to interest rates ceilings. As recent as 2013, the BCEAO, Central Bank of the West Africa Economic and Monetary Union, lowered the interest rate ceiling for MFIs to 24%. This is less than what many MFIs charge on standard loan products. Even if one disregards the interests of the MFI, it is ultimately the poor who are inadvertently penalised by a measure intended to protect them. "Ceilings"[37] reduce the gross yield and oblige MFIs to reduce expenditure on activities like maternal healthcare, literacy training, etc. or stop operating in remote areas.[38]

Another effect of interest rate ceilings is that they create a pent-up demand for loans. As a consequence, credit is not allocated by the market clearing price, but by personal connections, powerful lobbies and corruption. As the poor are not the ones with good connections, credit rationing will primarily benefit the better-off: exactly the opposite of what had been intended with the interest rate cap. Worse: a cap leads MFIs to finance projects that do not necessarily have the highest returns, a suboptimal growth effect. Interest rate ceilings also artificially lower the price of capital compared to labour, hence lead to the adoption of labour-saving technology. Since the interest cap indirectly also lowers the return on deposits, it discourages savings and encourages present consumption – again with a dampening effect on growth.[39]

To disentangle the controversy surrounding interest rate caps, it helps to distinguish between short- and long-term effects on MFIs. In the short-term, MFIs cannot compress any of the three cost components that influence the interest rate: in the short-term, the MFI cannot tangibly compress operating costs, nor get better conditions on its credit lines with donors to reduce capital costs. And it is impossible to bring about rapidly a tangible compression on the loan loss rate. In the short-term, the MFI is almost condemned to cut into its profit margin, which is the residual component of its gross yield and the only component over which it has direct control. The downside is that any plans to expand the network, innovate in products and delivery and so forth have to be put on hold. At best, the MFI makes an effort to appear to comply with the interest rate cap and hide any extra costs in commissions and fees.

In the longer-term, prospects are brighter: the MFI can lower its operating costs, for example, by raising staff productivity. It can reduce its refinancing costs by getting a licence to take deposits, a less costly resource. The MFI can also reduce loan losses by making its appraisal process more rigorous. And above all, the MFI can increase its overall loan portfolio, thus hoping to minimise average loan costs. In the longer-term, the MFI can also innovate in its product offer, by

98   *Public policy*

reviewing the costs of group loans vs individual loans and adjusting its lending technique accordingly, by analysing loan losses with regard to maturity and then focus on the less costly variant. It may expand or eliminate any graduation or collateral substitution approaches if found too costly. However, all these adjustments take time. In the short-run, an interest rate cap leaves a MFI no choice but to move into more lucrative markets, away from the delivery of very small costly loans.

Empirical studies[40] find that interest rate ceilings do not have the benefits expected in terms of consumer protection. Alternative public policy measures like incentives for more competition and product innovation, financial consumer protection, financial literacy and credit bureaus may have less of a political appeal, but are more effective. As in other markets, it is competition that is most likely to bring down the level of interest rates in microfinance in the short-term. The challenge for public policymakers is that the microfinance market is anything but a level playing field.

COMPETITION POLICY

Competition either among MFIs or between MFIs and banks should be beneficial for clients, suppliers and the microfinance market as a whole. However, studies on the effects of competition do not give a clear answer[41] to who actually benefits most. So, with over 20 years of operations on the ground, has competition in microfinance increased or – to the contrary – has it weakened and yielded monopolies? Using an indicator of price elasticity, a recent study[42] of 10 large microfinance markets found that the degree of competitiveness varies considerably. From 2003 to 2010 "India and Nicaragua had the most competitive microfinance loan markets, while competition among the MFIs in Bangladesh and Bolivia declined significantly and ... in other countries remained mostly unchanged."[43]

Competition should, in principle, drive down the interest rate. In some countries there has indeed been an increasing number of MFIs starting up and growing, without, however, leading to a change in the cost of credit to the client.[44] The effect on the interest rate seems to vary more with the type of microfinance institution: while NGO-type MFIs display the same loan rates and portfolio quality indicators, for-profit MFIs charge significantly lower rates and show improved portfolio quality (lower PARs).[45] When these two types of MFIs compete directly against each other in the same market, then the portfolio quality of NGO types of MFIs deteriorates. Other studies found a trend towards larger loan sizes[46] as the local microfinance market gets more competitive. This could be the effect of shrinking profit margins, which oblige MFIs to search for more profitable clients and reduce administrative costs per loan allocated. Cull, et al find that "competition, or potential competition from mainstream formal sector banks appears to steer microfinance institutions toward serving poorer customers."[47] The authors qualify the surprising finding by pointing out that the effect applies to settings where competition does not affect negatively the profitability of MFIs, presumably very large markets with niches.

On the other hand, competition between MFIs can also lead them to chase after clients and not share information about client-related risks. This could induce them to adopt more conservative lending practices, not necessarily to the benefit of smaller and poorer clients.[48] With pressure on profit margins, MFIs also tend to resort to opaque pricing, hiding the true cost of a loan in commissions and fees. Clients then pay more than what they believe they pay.[49]

The microfinance market is special, and that may explain why competition policy has not always had the expected effects. First, instead of having exclusively profit-maximising operators as in other markets, there are some that are and many others that are not. Many MFIs see themselves as social enterprises. Obviously, they respond to new entrants differently compared to profit-maximising firms. A second difference is the dependence of the entire microfinance market on donor funding (see Chapter 8), which influences the pricing decisions of MFIs – regardless of what happens in the market. Third, interest rate ceilings tie the hands of the managers of MFIs when they set the price. Lastly, there is the real or perceived price inelasticity of demand for microfinance products. A new entrant on the local market may thus not constitute an existential threat to the MFI's profit margin as one would expect.

A policy for healthy competition in microfinance would need to address these four specific challenges of microfinance markets. In addition, it would need to make the entry of new service providers easier, and it would arbitrate and moderate between MFIs with different business models and different degrees of subsidy dependence, and combat price fixing arrangements between oligopolistic MFIs. Competition policy would make sure there is no crowding-out by DFI-supported microfinance institutions at the expense of private and locally funded MFIs. It would put pressure on donors and international NGOs to coordinate the terms of their credit lines and the reporting requirements by MFIs; it would at the same time invest into risk-reducing financial infrastructure and steer donor money correspondingly: credit bureaux, transparency in pricing, financial literacy, common accounting and auditing standards and the collection and publication of market data. In other words, an ideal competition policy would operate from a higher level, out of reach of particular lobbies, having the common good at heart, disinterested and concerned for a level playing field for all types of MFIs.[50]

Needless to say, such a coherent, well-considered textbook policy for competition in microfinance does not exist. Instead, one sees short-term, politically driven interventions focusing on partial aspects of the microfinance market and affecting specific types of MFIs. One of the reasons why this is so is the fact that governments have – in addition to their roles in capacity building and rule-setting – an important funding role in microfinance. This complicates matters.

3. Funding as an instrument of public policy

Governments fund MFIs to provide resources for on-lending and to inject revenue to keep the entire operation going. To mobilise resources for their lending activities, MFIs can turn to governments, tap into the local financial market or negotiate a credit line with a foreign development bank (DFI) or a private investor (MIV). Government-sponsored funding (direct and via APEX funds) is not the number one debt resource of MFIs in Africa in volume, as the following graph[51] shows (Figure 10.1):

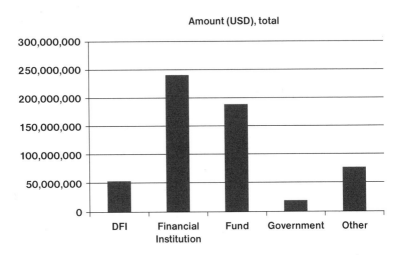

Figure 10.1 Sources of debt financing, sub-Sahara Africa 2011.

Public policy 101

But government loans (direct or through APEX funds) are less expensive than other sources (Figure 10.2).

In the graph before, the subsidy on the concessionary credit line is 5%. Often government funding is channelled via APEX funds, wholesale funds that refinance retail microfinance institutions (MFIs). CGAP identified 76 apexes in 46 countries.[52] The flow of resources via APEX mechanisms counts for as much as direct funding by donors and investors.[53] The existence of an Apex fund also has a political role: it signals that the government is committed to financial inclusion. Anecdotal evidence suggests that APEX funds do not disburse as much and as fast as expected, MFIs occasionally complain about bureaucratic handling of funding applications and reporting requirement, and above all, there is always the threat of political interference in the Apex fund management (Table 10.1).

The state can also directly intervene in the market by adding to the supply through its own agencies. Government-owned and -run retail institutions enter thus into direct competition with existing MFIs. This raises a number of issues. First, conflict of interest: the state cannot run its own MFI and at the same time supervise and regulate the microfinance sector. Second, the government may be motivated by considerations other than financial inclusion, for example by the desire to mobilise votes for an upcoming election. Third, if clients know that a MFI is government-owned, then they are less keen to pay back their loans. This moral hazard effect could spread to the entire

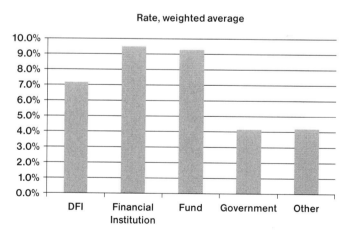

Figure 10.2 Average interest rate on credit lines to MFIs (weighted average, sub-Sahara Africa).

102 *Public policy*

Table 10.1 Top 10 wholesale funds (Apexes) 2009[54]

Apex	Country	Outstanding portfolio ($mio)
SIDBI	India	847
Nafinsa	Mexico	491
Bancoldex	Colombia	462
PKSF	Bangladesh	429
PPAF	Pakistan	137
BTS	Tunisia	117
Fedecredito	El Salvador	102
PCFC	Philippines	74
MISFA	Afghanistan	69
SFD	Egypt	67

microfinance sector. The fourth risk is price dumping. As governments tend to see only the short-term benefit in microfinance and not the longer-term institution-building perspective, the prices tend not to reflect actual costs, thus undercutting private MFIs that have their eyes set on longer-term institutional viability.

Less known instruments of public policy are fiscal measures of MFIs. Financial cooperatives in Kenya, for example, do not pay business tax on the interest income realised in their credit operations with members.[55] Since the interest spread is the main source of income for MFIs, this tax privilege for savings and credit cooperatives can be significant. Governments can decide to exempt entire types of MFIs (like NGOs and financial cooperatives) from taxes on profits, thus signalling that certain business models in microfinance have the favour of the government. Public policy can use fiscal tools to recognise and reward MFIs operating in remote areas or with very poor clients.

These instruments of public policy have in common that they can be used for the common good – equity in the access to the market, fair and transparent financing conditions for all, even the poor, as well as consumer protection, yet they can also be applied for particular interest groups and party politics. Obviously, this is not always openly acknowledged, but microfinance is just too inviting to be ignored by politicians seeking election or a reputation of caring for the poor.

Public policy in practice: politics and microfinance

Every five years farmers in a West African country have the pleasant surprise to see their debts towards the government-owned rural development bank reduced or cancelled by decision of the

Public policy 103

government party, in a pre-election period. After several debt cancellations in the past they adjust their repayment behaviour correspondingly.

In a large Latin American city, the incumbent mayor launched a "microfinance" institution one year before the municipal election. The sole purpose was to generate votes through the distribution of pseudo-credit (i.e. in actual fact mini-grants without any strings attached).

Faced with rising unemployment rates among college and university leavers and undergoing an austerity regime that implied a hiring stop in the public sector, the government of a North African country created a retail institution to distribute microcredit to university graduates. The clients were aware of the origin of the funds, i.e. the state. They largely defaulted, and the government refrained from collecting the loans due. As a result, the bank's capital evaporated.

These are three examples of "state activism," i.e. politically motivated uses of microfinance. There are many more. In fact, one gets the impression that a balanced, respectful and even-handed public policy approach to microfinance is rather exceptional. One does not win an election with arguments about institution-building, market development and the financial inclusion agenda in general. This is too abstract and complex and too difficult to explain. By contrast, the handout of small "loans" out of government funds, loans that everyone understands will never be reclaimed, is a much more effective argument in election times.

The hijacking of microfinance for political ends should not come as a surprise. It was the promoters of microfinance who claimed that it was a strategy that works for the poor. "State activism" is also driven by a certain jealousy vis-à-vis internationally supported NGO-MFIs that get all the attention for their good work fighting poverty. "Many worry that NGOs have become a shadow state and are undermining ... it... by providing essential services that are the domain of the state."[56] What better way for a Government to demonstrate its supremacy than clamp down on these good-doing MFIs, either by imposing interest rate ceilings in the name of consumer protection or by accusing foreign-supported MFIs to rip off innocent farmers or – even better – flood the market with cheap credit so that recalcitrant MFIs are forced out of business.

In conclusion, public policy for microfinance and financial inclusion is neither the steady and regular application of textbook theories,

104 *Public policy*

nor a continuous kidnapping of microfinance for party politics. It is a mixture of both, fluctuating in response to the occasional insolvency, debt crisis and election date. One and the same government may at one point in time decide on powerful market enhancing measures, and subsequently undo these effects and distort the market with politically driven decisions. On balance and over time, the zigzagging of public policy will not prevail over the inherent market dynamics and innovations in financial inclusion.

This could lead to the conclusion that public policy does not make any difference to the success of microfinance and financial inclusion. To the contrary: It does make a difference. It is not a coincidence that countries like Colombia and Peru that are credited with having a near-perfect "enabling environment"[57] for microfinance do very well on most indicators of financial inclusion.[58] Still, the question is valid: does public policy make a difference to the access and use of financial services by the poor, or is it actually the market and the individual institutions operating in it that make the difference? Or both? Or other factors? This is the focus of the next chapter on impact.

Notes

1 For a critique of this view, see J. Gershman and J. Morduch, Credit is not a right, Financial Access Initiative Research Framing Note, April 2011.
2 "Every person must be allowed to have a fair chance to improve his/her economic condition. This can be easily done by ensuring his/her right to credit. If the existing financial institutions fail to ensure that right, it is the obligation of the state and the world community to help find alternative financial institutions." Muhammad Yunus, Credit for self-employment: a fundamental human right. Background paper prepared for World Food Day, p. 6, 1986. Available at www.worldfooddayusa.org/Object.
3 www.cgap.org/blog/top-five-takeaways-cgap%E2%80%99s-2015-funders-survey.
4 The figures in this paragraph are from the CGAP Brief, Taking Stock-Recent Trends in International Funding for Financial Inclusion, 2016.
5 www.oecd.org/dac/stats/documentupload/Aid%20to%20agriculture%20and%20rural%20development%20data.pdf.
6 An overview of what individual countries are doing in this regard can be found under www.oecd.org/finance/financial-education/financial-education.htm.
7 AII, IAIS, Finmark Trust, FSB, Seminar on Financial Education: Challenges, Trends and Measures of Success in Supporting Financial Inclusion in Sub-Saharan Africa, 2016, Sandton, South Africa, p. 3.
8 OECD/INFE International Survey of Core Competencies of Adult Financial Literacy, Paris, 2016, p. 20.
9 IPA, Beyond the Classroom – Evidence on New Directions in Financial Education, Financial Inclusion Program Brief, IPA, January 2017; also:

Alejandro Drexler, Greg Fischer, and Antoinette Schoar, Keeping it simple: financial literacy and rules of thumb, *American Economic Journal: Applied Economics*, 2014, vol. 6, No. 2, pp. 1–31; also: Lisa Xu and Bilal Zia, *Financial Literacy around the World – An Overview of the Evidence with Practical Suggestions for the Way Forward*, World Bank, Development Research Group, Finance and Private Sector Development Team, June 2012, WPS6107.
10 www.credit-suisse.com/corporate/en/responsibility/economy-society/focus-themes/microfinance.html.
11 For example, by the Toronto Centre (www.torontocentre.org); the Financial Stability Institute of the BIS (www.bis.org/fsi); the Fletcher School Leadership Program for Financial Inclusion (sites.tufts.edu/flpfi).
12 CGAP Brief, Taking Stock – Recent Trends in International Funding for Financial Inclusion, 2016.
13 This section examines only regulation of MFIs. There is more to regulation for financial inclusion. Portfolio quotas, for example, that are instituted in some countries to oblige banks to set aside a given percentage of the entire loan portfolio for a sector considered underserved: microenterprises, rural enterprises, start-ups and so forth. Another example for directed public policy for financial inclusion are "smart" reserve requirements that reward banks with more favourable terms provided they can demonstrate that they reached a target for underserved sectors.

More country-level data can be obtained from the Microfinance Gateway under: The Regulation and Supervision Resource Center www.cgap.org/regulation.
14 Three major doctrines: adjust and accommodate under existing banking supervision and regulation (example Bolivia); create specific framework for MFI supervision and regulation (UMOEA/BCEAO); and lastly, self-regulation modelled on the cooperative governance (Philippines and South Africa, WOCCU, Content Guide ..., part XIII, p. 39). See for more on regulation and supervision of microfinance institutions: BIS, Microfinance Supervision versus Banking Supervision, Basel 2010; CGAP, Regulating and Supervision of MFIs – Stabilizing a New Financial Market, Focus Note no. 4, August 1996; CGAP, The Rush to Regulate: Legal Frameworks for Microfinance, Occasional Papers 4, 2000; CGAP, Regulation and Supervision of Microfinance, Donor Brief 12, 2003; CGAP, A Guide to Regulation and Supervision of Microfinance – Consensus Guidelines, 2012; S. Berenbach, and C. Churchill, Regulation and Supervision of Microfinance Institutions: Experience from Latin America, Asia and Africa, Occasional Paper No. 1, Microfinance Network, Washington, D.C 1997; EIU, The Global Microscope 2016 – The enabling environment for financial inclusion (www.eiu.com/landing/Global-Microscope); L. Lhériau, Précis de la Réglementation de la Microfinance, AFD, 2009.
15 Bank for International Settlement, Basel Committee on Banking Supervision, Microfinance activities and the Core Principles for Effective Banking Supervision, February 2010; also: T. Fisher, et al., *Beyond Microcredit – Putting Development back into Microfinance*, London 2002; S. Staschen, Regulatory Requirements for Microfinance, GTZ, Division 41 Economic Development and Employment Promotion, Eschborn, 2003
16 BIS, op. cit., pp. 12–29.

106 *Public policy*

17 D. Porteous, D. Collins, and J. Abrams, Prudential Regulation in Microfinance, Financial Access Initiative Policy Framing Note, 2010, p. 3.
18 www.bou.or.ug/bou/media/from_the_bank/Minimum_Capital_Requirements_FIs_Supervised_by_BoU.html.
19 www.ceditalk.com/2016/12/minimum-capital-requirements-for-financial-institutions-in-ghana/.
20 See Table 3 in S. Staschen, p. 24.
21 www.ifmr.co.in/blog/2016/06/30/a-comparison-of-capital-requirements-for-microfinance-and-housing-finance-institutions.
22 BCEAO/UEMOA, Loi portant réglementation des institutions Mutualistes ou Coopératives d'Epargne et de Crédit, (Loi PARMEC), Dakar, Septembre 1993.
23 CGAP, Consensus Guidelines, op. cit., p. 24.
24 CGAP, Measuring Results of Microfinance Institutions – Minimum Indicators That Donors and Investors Should Track – A Technical Guide, 2009.
25 A more flexible approach is proposed in: WB and IMF, Financial Sector Assessment – A Handbook, Chapter 7: Rural and Microfinance Institutions: Regulatory and Supervisory Issues, 2005, p. 196.
26 R. Cull, A. Demirguc-Kunt, J. Morduch, Microfinance Trade-Offs: Regulation, Competition and Financing, *The Handbook of Microfinance*, p. 152.
27 Idem, p. 153.
28 L. Lhériau, p. 92.
29 www.smartcampaign.org/storage/documents/Pocantico_Declaration.pdf.
30 www.smartcampaign.org/.
31 www.smartcampaign.org/about/campaign-endorsers#MFI; this is a much more than the MFIs posted on the MIX market (over 1400).
32 Measures that affect capital costs and margins in banking – and thus microfinance – are:

   Open Market Operations: the purchase and sale of securities in the open market by a central bank with the intention to keep interest rates down and encourage investment, production and employment. MFIs are not directly affected by this monetary measure, but it is easy to see that in a low interest rate market environment MFIs that charge 30% or more annual rates of interest tend to be noticed.

   Discount rate: the interest rate charged to commercial banks and other depository institutions when they approach the central bank for a credit line. Obviously, the discount rate determines what a bank can charge the borrower client, and thus its gross margin. While few MFI need to go for this form of refinancing in contrast to banks, the discount rate signals to attentive MFIs the gross margin that their competitors enjoy or have to cope with.

   Reserve requirements: funds that a depository institution must hold in reserve at the Central Bank. "The reserve ratio depends on the amount of net transactions accounts at the depository institution." Due to modest volumes in the operations of microfinance institutions, MFIs are not (yet) required to deposit a given percentage of their assets with the central bank.
33 https://opportunity.org/content/News/Publications/Knowledge%20Exchange/2011%20Sub-Saharan%20Africa%20Regional%20Snapshot.pdf, slide 23.

Public policy 107

34 S.M. Maimbo and C. Alejandra Henriquez Gallegos, Interest Rate Caps around the World Still Popular, but a Blunt Instrument, Finance and Markets Global Practice Group, Policy Research Working Paper 7070, WB, October 2014, p. 6.
35 S.M. Maimbo, et al., op. cit., p. 10; see also: H. Miller, *Interest Rate Caps and Their Impact on Financial Inclusion*. Nathan Associates, EPS Peaks, 2013.
36 R. Rosenberg, S. Gaul, W. Ford and O. Tomilova, Microcredit Interest Rates and Their Determinants 2004–2011, Access to Finance Forum, Reports by CGAP and Its Partners, No. 7, June 2013, p. 21.
37 In Cambodia, the National Bank established an interest rate cap of 18% on loans provided by microfinance institutions. The impact of this new regulation remains to be seen but it is expected to be detrimental to financial inclusion and pricing transparency." SYMBIOTICS, Monthly Report March 2017.
38 CGAP, The Role of Governments in Microfinance, Donor Brief No. 19, June 2004. This reflected in a comparison of microfinance penetration ratios in countries with and without interest rate caps: CGAP, Interest Rate Ceilings and Microfinance – The Story so Far, Occasional Paper 9, 2004, p. 6. Actually, the opposite could also be the case: it could be that the higher microfinance penetration in some markets exerts competitive pressures on interest rates and makes interest rate caps unnecessary.
39 W. James, Credit Rationing, Rural savings and financial policy in developing countries, ADB Economic Staff Papers, No. 13, p. 8.
40 S.M. Maimbo, op. cit., p. 12.
41 McIntosh and Wydick (2005) claim that competition may lower the borrower selection standards, weaken bank-customer relationships and enhance multiple borrowing and loan defaults. J. Schicks and R. Rosenberg (2011) argue that MFIs' outreach and loan portfolio performance in general have declined due to competition and clients are now more prone to over-indebtedness. Quoted in A.K. Kar (2016). Measuring competition in microfinance markets: a new approach, *International Review of Applied Economics*, vol. 30, No. 4, pp. 423–440.
42 A.K. Kar, Measuring competition in microfinance markets: a new approach, *International Review of Applied Economics*, vol. 30, No. 4, 423–440.
43 Kar. op. cit., p. 427.
44 D. Porteous, Competition and Microcredit Interest Rates, CGAP Focus Note 33, 2006.
45 G. Baquero, M. Hamadi, and A. Heinen, Competition, loan rates and information dispersion in microcredit markets, ESMT Working Papers 12-02, 2012, pp. 4 and 26.
46 F. Olivares-Polanco, *Commercializing microfinance and deepening outreach? Empirical evidence from Latin America*, U Pittsburgh, 2003, p. 21.
47 R. Cull, A. Demirgüc-Kunt and J. Morduch, Microfinance Trade-Offs: Regulation, Competition and Financing, *Handbook of Microfinance*, p. 143.
48 C. McIntosh and B. Wydick, Competition and Microfinance, *Journal of Development Economics*, vol. 78, 2005, p. 271.
49 C. Waterfield, *Transparency in Microfinance – The Client Perspective*, presentation at UMM, Frankfurt, 2012.
50 D. Porteous, op. cit., p. 14.

108 Public policy

51 MIX and CGAP Analysis of Key Trends, Sub Saharan Africa Microfinance Regional Snapshot, 2012, slide 28.
52 CGAP, A New Look at Microfinance Apexes, Focus Note 80, June 2012, p. 1.
53 CGAP Brief, APEXES – an important source of local funding, March 2010.
54 CGAP, A New Look at Microfinance Apexes, Focus Note 80, June 2012, p. 3.
55 Julius Mwatu, Financial Reporting for Saccos Tax Planning & Management, Institute of Certified Public Accountants of Kenya (ICPAK).
56 A. Dowla, Political interference in microfinance, *Enterprise Development and Microfinance*, Vol. 26, No. 4, December 2015, p. 359.
57 The EIU (Global Microscope 2016) defines "enabling environment" with the help of 12 indicators: (1) government support for financial inclusion, (2) regulatory and supervisory capacity for financial inclusion, (3) prudential regulation, (4) regulation and supervision of credit portfolios, (5) regulation and supervision of deposit-taking activities, (6) regulation of insurance targeting low-income populations, (7) regulation and supervision of branches and agents, (8) requirements for non-regulated lenders, (9) electronic payments, (10) credit-reporting systems, (11) market conduct rules, and (12) dispute resolution mechanisms.
58 www.worldbank.org/en/programs/globalfindex.

11 Impact

Of all development strategies, microfinance is probably the one that is the most concerned about its impact. Conversations about microfinance mostly focus on claims and evidence of changes in the lives of the poor. Going by the debates at conferences and in journals, one gets the impression that the microfinance industry is obsessed with its impact, i.e. changes in the situation of clients that can be causally attributed to the access and use of financial services. Most controversies have to do with the selection of the right variables, measurement issues, the dimensions and levels of impact and assessment methodologies. There is a wealth of impact evaluations.[1] The evidence is mixed with some studies confirming positive or negative effects on some metrics, but with every wave of experimental analyses – randomised or not – the complexity of causal linkages becomes ever more obvious between access to and use of financial services and changes in the welfare of individuals, households and villages.

We have seen that most microfinance institutions are still subsidised, in one way or another. Donor agencies therefore continue to play an important role. As donor agencies are accountable to parliamentary scrutiny, they must provide evidence that the grants to MFIs are well spent. Private investors in microfinance – commercial and social – also want to see the evidence of financial and social returns.

Impact of what?

What does one actually mean by impact "of microfinance"? The effect of a specific financial product – presumably credit? There are various types of credit: emergency loans, consumer loans or rather loans that make an income generating activity possible or more lucrative, which one of these? All microloan products? And why stop at microcredit, why not include in the analysis any service and product offered by

110 *Impact*

a microfinance institution? Surely it makes sense to widen the scope to other products and financial services like deposits, insurance, payments, micro-leasing and non-financial services.

Instead of a focus on products, impact assessments can also scrutinise particular techniques to deliver these products, notably by groups of clients, and how these operational choices affect the incomes and well-being of clients. Many empirical studies have looked at the comparative merits and weaknesses of group-lending versus individual lending.[2] One can examine the effects of different lending techniques in different MFIs operating in the same market, compare the performance of group lending versus individual lending in one and the same MFI, or take a longitudinal perspective and track the effects on clients as a result of switching from one lending technique to another.

"Impact of microfinance" obviously is a minefield complicated by the heterogeneity of institutions providing microfinance. Microfinance institutions affect the lives and work of their clients in different ways. The types of institutions that offer microfinance differ in their focus on particular target populations, the range of services offered and their accessibility. Some MFIs have the ambition to reach the poorest of the poor,[3] while others target clients near and even above the poverty line. At the same time, even the most commercially oriented MFIs like Compartamos affirm a commitment to reduce poverty.[4]

Naturally there is not a single, unique impact of all MFIs, but rather a complex web of conflicting and reinforcing effects. The analysis at the level of microfinance institutions is thus challenging enough. Few studies attempted aggregation and look at the overall impact on microfinance markets and different regulatory, supervisory, competitive and fiscal regimes – not to speak of the ultimate aggregation, i.e. the global impact of microfinance on the poor in terms of the Sustainable Development Goals. This has led some authors to exasperate: "ultimately the question does microfinance work? Is impossible to answer because microfinance is not a single tool but a collection of tools."[5]

Impact on what?[6]

The use of microloans can lead to higher productivity and income, more or less child labour, more or less leisure, more self-confidence in a woman entrepreneur, access to input markets, recruitment of labour from outside the family, over-indebtedness and so forth. The list of dependent variables is daunting.[7] Instead of taking up one variable after the other and presenting in every instance the state of knowledge in the impact assessment literature, we focus on the – admittedly

Impact 111

elusive – concept of poverty, because that was the claim made in the early days of microfinance, namely that it would make a dent on poverty and even reduce it so effectively that one could even envisage to "...to build museums to display (the) horrors (of poverty) to future generations."[8]

Poverty encompasses multiple dimensions, all of which have been examined in impact assessments: *financial* like assets, income[9] and over-indebtedness,[10] *economic* dimensions like employment,[11] productivity and displacement effects and the diversification of activities in household-enterprises, finally *social* dimensions like empowerment, vulnerability, food security and education[12] and *environmental* aspects.[13] For each of these variables, there exists a host of indicators.[14]

Probing into any of these dimensions in isolation would clearly not capture the full picture of impact: there may have been a positive impact on the family's overall financial situation, but at the expense of having to withdraw children from school to take care of an income-generating activity. To get a fair and balanced idea, one would need to look at poverty in all its dimensions at the same time. And presumably not just of a single family and household-enterprise, but at the multiple ways it interacts with other household-enterprises in the same community.[15] Participation in a microfinance scheme could conceivably enhance the standing of a family in its neighbourhood, just as it could conceivably trigger pressure in the community to share any benefits that may have accrued from its status as a client of a MFI.

Initial claims

The adoption of the Millennium Development Goals by the UN in 2005 was a golden opportunity to point out the manifold benefits of microfinance.[16]

> Empirical evidence shows that, among the poor, those participating in microfinance programs who had access to financial services were able to improve their well-being—both at the individual and household level—much more than those who did not have access to financial services.[17]

This statement would seem to confirm the original claims of microfinance. It is backed up by examples from real-life MFIs, like Grameen in Bangladesh, where the incomes of members were 43% higher than incomes in non-programme villages, or SHARE in India, which saw

112   *Impact*

half of its clients graduate out of poverty, or FINCA in El Salvador, where the weekly income of clients increased on average by 145%.

The news was equally encouraging when looking at the impact on education:

> In Bangladesh, almost all girls in Grameen client households had some schooling, compared to 60% of girls in non-client households.... Basic competency in reading, writing, and arithmetic among children 11–14 years old in BRAC member households increased from 12% in 1992 to 24% in 1995, compared to only 14% for children in non-member households. ...In Peru, Acción Communitaria del Peru-borrower households spent 20% more on schooling for their children than non-borrower households.[18]

And in health, the findings were equally positive:

> In Bangladesh, Grameen clients showed a higher rate of contraceptive use (59%) than non-clients (43%). ... In Uganda, 95% of clients of FOCCAS ...engaged in some practices for improved health and nutrition of their children compared to 72% of non-clients.[19]

These cases are based on longitudinal analysis of panel data. Other illustrations of this approach are the AIMS studies commissioned by USAID in the late 1990s and early 2000s that probed into the impact of "microenterprise services"[20] using surveys of clients of SEWA in India, Mibanco in Peru and Zambuko Trust in Zimbabwe at two points in time (at an interval of two years) and identified non-clients with similar socioeconomic profiles in the neighbourhood. Net income gains were observed in India and Peru, but not in Zimbabwe – always in comparison to the respective control groups.

Pitt and Khandker (1998)[21] and Khandker (2005)[22] collected extensive household data in Bangladesh and found positive impacts of the use of microcredit on incomes, especially for women clients. However, their findings were subsequently questioned by Morduch and Roodman (2009)[23] and led to an extensive methodological discussion about omitted variables and hidden selection bias.

By most non-randomised measures, microfinance seemed to have turned out just to be the miracle that it had been claimed to be: capable of addressing multiple aspects of poverty and deprivation, and at the same time reaching out to millions of poor people. However, with closer scrutiny, it turned out that the causal link between improved health, educational and income status could have been the result of access to and use of microfinance, but not necessarily so. The beneficial impact could also have been caused by other factors that were not controlled for. The aforementioned case studies tracked indicators of clients of a single MFI over time or compared a group of microfinance users with non-users. The drawbacks of this type of impact assessment is that the outcome is distorted by the constitution of the groups compared. By looking at households that are clients of the MFI, one may overlook factors that explain not just their participation in the microfinance programme but also the difference in benefits generated.

Programme participants join for reasons that are unobserved and that explain why they do better than non-participants. Self-selection by programme participants can lead to overstating the beneficial impact of microfinance.[24] "Those households that get access to credit are not likely to be a random draw from the population. Their very success in accessing credit is an indicator of otherwise unmeasured abilities."[25] A survey of 87 rural communities in Bangladesh 1991–1992 (BRAC and Grameen clients) showed "high-profit households to be more likely to participate in Grameen Bank ... (with) ... large positive and significant total effects of participation on self-employment profits."[26] A similar error in the selection of seemingly homogeneous villages can occur if some features are overlooked, for example differences in the access to infrastructure or contagion and spillover effects between the treatment and the control group. Self-selection[27] and the resulting overestimation of impact can be dealt with in an experimental design, which allocates individual households or entire villages in treatment or control groups randomly and in large numbers. Ideally household-enterprises in both groups would be identical in all respects – except one: participation (or not) in the microfinance programme.[28]

From correlation to causation: randomised experimental impact assessments

Three initiatives by researchers based at MIT, NYU and Yale promoted the application of experimental research to microfinance from the late 1990s onwards: Financial Access Initiative,[29] Innovations for Poverty Action[30] and the Jameel Poverty Action Lab.[31] In the subsequent decade, an increasing number of impact assessments were carried out that sought to correct for the selection and other biases.[32] A large number of studies emerged that used randomisation in experimental (RCTs) and quasi-experimental approaches (difference-in-difference, instrumental variables, regression discontinuity, propensity score matching, pipeline approach). In January 2015, the American

114 *Impact*

Economic Journal – Applied Economics[33] presented the findings of six randomised evaluations of microcredit interventions in Bosnia-Herzegovina, Ethiopia, India, Mexico, Mongolia, and Morocco. These RCT studies found (i) relatively low take-up rates; (ii) increases in credit overall; (iii) increases in business activity, but (iv) little impact on profits, income or consumption (Figure 11.1).[34]

Randomised control trials require substantial household survey data, which makes the exercise relatively expensive. Because of costs and a certain reluctance of MFIs to get involved in a heavy data gathering exercise for too long, the time horizon of RCTs is rarely more than two or three years. This means that a RCT cannot capture changes in a household-enterprise that take longer to materialise.[35] Also, randomisation implies that households assigned to the control group cannot benefit from the microfinance product or innovation that is offered to the treatment group. Some MFIs find this exclusion unacceptable for ethical reasons. In fact, on the ground, it is hard to avoid contamination. Another shortcoming of RCTs is that the findings are not necessarily replicable to other contexts. Like other impact assessment techniques, RCTs have only limited validity tied to a particular location, market, period and type of MFI.

The impact of microcredit: 6 RCTs

	Bosnia	Ethiopia	India	Mexico	Mongolia	Morocco
↑ = (+) significant ✖ = insignificant ↓ = (−) significant	Men & women, individual loans, $1,800, 22% APR	Men & women, group liability, $500, 12% APR	Women only, group liability, $600, 24% APR	Women only, group liability, $450, 110% APR	Women only, individual & group, $700, 27% APR	Men & women, group liability, $1,100, 15% APR
Credit access	↑	↑	↑	↑	↑	↑
Business Activity	↑	↑	↑	↑	✖	↑
Income	✖	✖	✖	✖	✖	✖
Consumption	↓	↓	✖	✖	↑	✖
Social effects	✖	✖	✖	↑	✖	✖

Figure 11.1 The impact of microcredit: findings of six randomised control trials.

Impact 115

As of late, the controversy about the "right" approach to impact assessments in microfinance has led to a consensus that a combination of methods is most likely to do justice to the large variety of microfinance interventions and outcomes. As an illustration, the University of Bath developed the "QiIP," Qualitative Impact Protocol, as a complement to experimental designs and as a "simple and cost-effective way to gather, analyse and present feedback from intended beneficiaries about significant drivers of change in their lives."[36] Also, longer-term in-depth client surveys – as applied in 2010 in Bangladesh by P. Davis[37] for IFPRI – can enrich and complement RCTs in the same location.

An original and intensive method to generate client data potentially reflecting impact are "financial diaries." In contrast to snapshot interviews, Rutherford et al. interviewed hundreds of households every two weeks to track their financial transactions in Bangladesh in 2000, India in 2001 and South Africa in 2003.[38]

Meta-evaluations

The 2011 overview of several randomised and non-randomised reviews by Odell[39] concludes that given the variety of microfinance tools and local market environments it is impossible to answer generally the question of whether microfinance works. While the effects on existing microbusinesses are reported as positive, the effects on incomes, poverty, education, health and women's status are less clear.

In their review of 10 RCTs carried out between 2008 and 2011, Bauchet et al. observe diversity in the needs of poor households and the degree of effectiveness with which MFIs respond to these needs – in credit design, micro-savings, micro-insurance or financial literacy training.[40] A common thread in these 10 RCTs is the heterogeneity of needs, abilities and capacities with regard to opportunities, risk mitigation and protection against shocks.

In their 2011 review, Duvendack et al. analysed 58 papers (RCTs and quasi-experimental designs) and arrived at the conclusion that "almost all impact evaluations of microfinance suffer from weak methodologies and inadequate data."[41]

The systematic review of 15 rigorous evaluations of the impact of microfinance in Africa[42] published in 2012 (selected out of a pool of 69 relevant pieces of analysis) concluded that it was impossible to synthesise the findings for the entire continent and for all intervention types of microfinance. The 15 studies reviewed observed both positive and negative impacts of microcredit on the incomes of poor people, regardless of the lending methodology. Microcredit and micro-savings

116 *Impact*

appear to have a positive impact on poor people's savings, health and food security.[43] However, as regards school enrolment, the evidence is mixed, with participants in some microcredit programmes being obliged to take children out of school.[44]

In 2016, Buera et al.[45] compared the six RCTs of the special 2015 issue of the AEJ mentioned before with two additional RCTs and confirmed the finding that existing entrepreneurs benefitted more from the intervention than those inclined to start a new activity. Some studies observe a positive effect on rural wages as individuals chose to take up microloans rather than work as unskilled agricultural labourers. Whether there is substitution of bank and informal loans is not a consistent finding across these studies.

Critical factors

Demonstrating impact in development is never simple, not just in microfinance. One needs lots of household data, often on sensitive issues – hence, likely to be biased – and one needs long time series data to control for variations over time. The participation of the poor in development projects is likely to be distorted by self-selection. There are ethical issues whenever one separates the poor in treatment and control groups as required by randomised control trials (RCT) and is forced to withhold benefits from the latter that are made available to the former. Selection bias, attribution issues and other challenges also affect impact assessments of schooling programmes, rural development or maternal health projects.

The difficulties to establish a causality between access to and use of microfinance and changes in the incomes and other metrics of poverty have to do with the peculiar features of the most common client type in microfinance: the household-enterprise. Whether a microloan is effectively used to bolster the working capital of a household-enterprise, or whether it is used for some other purpose like school or medical fees, is difficult to tell because of the fungibility of money. Also, the household-enterprise operates with a bundle of income-generating activities. In such a household, it is difficult to track the flow of a microfinance loan. It may have been used for the activity signalled by the client; it may however also have been used for other activities or to pay back a debt.

There are other complications that stem from the peculiar set-up of household-enterprises:

a   A household-enterprise consists of one or several families. Microfinance institutions, on the other hand, make contracts with individuals. Some MFIs are in fact rather restrictive in whom they consider eligible: women versus men, young versus adult, agriculture versus other activities, ownership of land or other assets not exceeding a given threshold and so forth. In a household-enterprise, some individuals may thus be eligible but others not. In settings of pent-up demand for microloans, this has led to situations where some members of the family are pushed to figure as the contracting party, without having any control within the family over the use of the loan.[46]

b   There are different poverty levels. Some MFIs try to make sure to reach household-enterprises at the desired poverty level, while others have less specific targets.[47] Household-enterprises consisting of many adults and children are sometimes difficult to classify in particular poverty levels. A microloan may positively affect only one activity without improving the well-being of the household-enterprise as a whole. An impact assessment that examines only the productivity changes in a "micro-entrepreneurial" activity would thus overstate the impact.

c   The research on "Financial Diaries" showed that the clients of MFIs manage a multitude of informal and formal financial transactions – in parallel to their dealings with the MFI. The variety of instruments reflects the multiple needs of household-enterprise in consumption, risk protection and business. In most situations, clients have a choice between their MFI or some informal financial service provider – or another MFI. Clients can and do "drop out." Wright found in East Africa[48] that dropouts signal that clients are in difficulties. This tends to lead to an overestimation of beneficial impact, since it is the successful clients who remain in the data set.

Returning to the initial promises and claims, the evidence is less clear: "30 years into the microfinance movement we have little solid evidence that it improves the lives of clients in measurable ways" (Roodman/ Murdoch 2009). This sounds sobering. However, this observation can be read as an appeal to do more research on impact. Rosenberg comes to a similar conclusion. Rather than volunteering generalisations about the benefits or damages of microfinance, he admits that "we simply do not know yet whether microcredit or other forms of microfinance are helping to lift millions out of poverty."

Some of the changes induced by the access to and use of finance may take place without being necessarily visible to researchers. While the transformative power of access to finance is still to be proven, there is a consensus that microfinance has helped many poor to smooth their

118 *Impact*

consumption. It has also reached scale, i.e. outreach to over several hundred million people near the poverty line, and there is a range of specialised robust institutions that have weathered already a few crises and sometimes done better than banks. Microfinance has triggered innovations in products and delivery and continues to do so. Other domains in finance, notably impact investing, are adopting lessons learnt in microfinance.

It is true that impact assessments of microfinance, whether qualitative or quantitative, experimental or non-experimental, do not show a spectacular improvement in the lives of millions, but rather a few success stories here and there and for the vast majority simply a more efficient way to manage household and microenterprise finances. The continued use of microfinance by millions of household-enterprises in low-income countries would suggest that microfinance cannot be that bad.

That microfinance falls short of being a panacea can surprise only those who believe in panaceas. Microfinance is still around and will be in demand in the foreseeable future. Thanks to its hybrid position between commercial and social goals, there will always be questions about the impact of microfinance, whether from donors or governments or "impact investors."

Notes

1 A. Banerjee, et al. (2010). *The Miracle of Microfinance? Evidence from a Randomized Evaluation*, J-PAL and MIT; J. Bauchet and A. Dalal, Randomized experiments in microfinance, *Microfinance Insights*, vol. 12, 2009; J. Bauchet, et al. (2011). Latest Findings from Randomized Evaluations of Microfinance, Access to Finance Forum, No. 2, (CGAP, FAI, IPA, ALPAL); B. Coleman, The impact of group lending in Northeast Thailand, *Journal of Development Economics*, vol. 60, 1999, pp. 105–141; F.J. Buera, J. Kaboski, and Y. Shin, Taking Stock of the Evidence on Micro-Financial Interventions, NBER Working Paper No. 22674, September 2016; D. Collins, et al., Portfolios of the poor: how the world's poor live on $2 a day, 2009; J. Copestake, N. Goldberg, and D. Karlan (2009). Randomised control trials are the best way to measure impact of microfinance programmes and improve microfinance product designs, *Enterprise Development and Microfinance*, vol. 20, No. 3, pp. 167–176; B. Crépon, et al., Impact of microcredit in rural areas of Morocco: evidence from randomized evaluation, J-PAL Working Paper, 2011; E. Duflo, Field experiments in development economics, World Congress of the Econometric Society, 2006; E. Duflo and K. Kremer, Use of randomization in the evaluation of development effectiveness, Paper prepared for the World Bank Operations Evaluation Department (OED) Conference on Evaluation and Development Effectiveness, Washington, 2003; E. Duflo, A. Banerjee, R. Glennerster, and C.G. Kinnan, The Miracle of Microfinance? Evidence from a Randomized Evaluation, Working Paper 18950, NBER, May 2013; M. Duvendack, R. Palmer-Jones, J.G. Copestake, L. Hooper,

Impact 119

Y. Loke, and N. Rao, What is the evidence of the impact of microfinance on the well-being of poor people? Research Report. London, 2011: EPPI-Centre, Social Science Research Unit, Institute of Education, University of London; X. Giné and D. Karlan, Peer monitoring and enforcement: long term evidence from microcredit lending groups with and without joint liability, Yale University, Economic Growth Center Working Paper, 2008; N. Goldberg, *Measuring the Impact of Microfinance: Taking Stock of What We Know*, Grameen Foundation USA Publication series, 2005; N. Goldberg and D. Karlan, Impact of credit: how to measure impact and improve operations too, FAI/IPA, 2008; N. Goldberg, D. Karlan, and J. Zinman, Randomized trials for strategic innovation in retail finance, FAI/IPA, 2008; D. Karlan and N. Goldberg, The impact of microfinance: a review of methodological issues, FAI, 2006; D. Karlan and J. Zinman, Expanding microenterprise credit access: using randomized supply decisions to estimate the impacts in Manila, 2010; J. Morduch, Is microfinance research as bad as medical research? CGAP Blog, 5 January 2011; K. Odell, *Measuring the Impact of Microfinance – Taking another Look*, Grameen Foundation Publication, 2010, p. 6; D. Roodman and J. Morduch, The impact of microcredit on the poor in Bangladesh: revisiting the evidence, FAI and NYU Wagner, 2009; R. Rosenberg, Does microcredit really help poor people? CGAP Focus Note No. 59, 2010; C. van Rooyen, R. Stewart, and T.de Wet, The impact of microfinance in sub-Saharan Africa: a systematic review of the evidence, *World Development*, vol. 40, No. 11, 2012, pp. 2249–2262.

2 S. Navajas, et al., Microcredit and the poorest of the poor: theory and evidence from Bolivia, *World Development*, vol. 28, No. 2, 2000, pp. 333–346: "group lenders in Bolivia reach the poorest better than individual lenders" (p. 334); X. Gine and D. Karlan, Group versus individual liability: short and long term evidence from Philippine microcredit lending groups, *Journal of Development Economics*, vol. 107, 2014, pp. 65–83; O. Attanasio, et al., Group lending versus individual lending in Mongolia in "The Impacts of Microfinance: Evidence from Joint-Liability Lending in Mongolia." *American Economic Journal: Applied Economics*, vol. 7, No. 1, 2015, 90–122.

3 S. Hashemi and R. Rosenberg, Graduating the Poorest into Microfinance: Linking Safety Nets and Financial Services, CGAP Focus Note 34, February 2006.

4 "We are a bank that generates social, economic and human value. We are committed to people; we generate opportunities for development within low-income segments of the population. These opportunities are based on innovative and efficient, large scale business models and on transcendental values which generate an internal and external culture while building lasting relationships and trust, therefore contributing to a better world." Mission statement on the MIX market.

5 K. Odell, *Measuring the Impact of Microfinance – Taking another Look*, Grameen Foundation USA, 2010, p. 6.

6 The impact on the local financial market is not dealt with here, i.e. changes in the operations of other financial service providers, whether informal or formal, as a result of the entry of MFIs. This is an important form of impact but would be beyond the scope of this book.

7 G. Schrieder and M. Sharma, Impact of Finance on Poverty Reduction and social capital formation, *Savings and Development*, vol. XXIII, No.1, 1999, p. 187.

120 Impact

8 M. Yunus, *Creating a World without Poverty: Social Business and the Future of Capitalism*, Public Affairs, New York, 2007.

9 E. Dunn and G. Arbuckle, Microcredit and microenterprise performance: impact evidence from Peru, *SED*, vol. 12, No. 4, 2001, p. 31; M. Hossein and C. Diaz, Reaching the poor with effective Microcredit: evaluation of a Grameen bank Replication in the Philippines, CARD Conference, Los Banos, 1997, p. 15; D. Hulme and P. Mosley, *Finance against Poverty*, London and New York 1996, vol. I, p. 185.

10 A. Diagne, Impact of access to credit on income and food security in Malawi, FCND Discussion Paper 46, 1998; D. Hulme and P. Mosley, *Finance against Poverty*, London and New York, 1996.

11 S. Khandker, H. Samad, and Z. Khan, Income and employment effects of microcredit programs: village-level evidence from Bangladesh, *Journal of Development Studies*, vol. 35, No. 2, December 1998.

12 N. Goldberg, *Measuring the Impact of Microfinance: Taking Stock of What We Know*, Grameen Foundation USA, 2005; C. Dunford, Sustainable Integration of Microfinance with Education in child survival, reproductive health and HIV/AIDS prevention for the poorest entrepreneurs, in S. Daley-Harris (ed.), *Pathways out of poverty*, 2002.

13 Dunn and Hossein, op. cit.

14 S. Carvalho and H. White, Indicators for Monitoring Poverty Reduction, World Bank Discussion Paper 254, 1994, pp. 26–37.

15 D. Hulme and P. Mosley, op. cit., p. 109.

16 E. Littlefield, J. Morduch, and S. Hashemi, Is Microfinance an Effective Strategy to Reach the Millennium Development Goals? CGAP/MIX, Focus note 24, January 2003.

17 CGAP, Microfinance and the Millennium Development Goals, Donor Brief 9, December 2002; also CGAG/MIX Blog 2003.

18 CGAP/MIX Blog 2003.

19 Idem.

20 See B. Armendariz and J. Morduch, *The Economics of Microfinance*, 2nd edition, MIT, 2010, p. 210.

21 M. Pitt and S. Khandker, The Impact of group-based credit programs on poor households in Bangladesh: does the gender of participants matter? *Journal of Political Economy*, vol. 106, No. 5, 1998, pp. 958–996.

22 S. Khandker, Microfinance and poverty: evidence using panel data from Bangladesh, *World Bank Economic Review*, vol. 19, 2005, pp. 263–286.

23 For a detailed account of the controversy, see for example D. Roodman, *Due Diligence*, op. cit., pp. 160–165.

24 By as much as 100%, if the outcome analysed is enterprise profit (S.M. Mc Kernan).

25 P. Honohan, Financial Sector Policy and the Poor – Selected Findings and Issues, World Bank Working Paper 43, 2004, p. 27.

26 S.M. Mc Kernan, The impact of microcredit programs on self employment profits: do non-credit program aspects matter? *Review of Economics and Statistics*, vol. 84, No. 1, February 2002, p. 109.

27 B. Coleman, op. cit., S.M. McKernan, op. cit.

28 J. Morduch points out that given the expansion of microfinance in some countries like Bangladesh, it has become difficult to find proper control groups.

Impact 121

29 Housed by the NYU Wagner School, the FAI is a research centre focused on exploring how financial services can better meet the needs and improve the lives of poor households. It was founded in 2006 by economists Jonathan Morduch, Dean Karlan, and Sendhil Mullainathan.

30 Founded in 2002 by Dean Karlan, the IPA Innovations for Poverty Action (IPA) is a "research and policy nonprofit that discovers and promotes effective solutions to global poverty problems."

31 The Poverty Action Lab at MIT, founded in 2003 by A. Banerjee, E. Duflo, and S. Mullainathan aims at promoting "the use of randomized evaluations, to train others in rigorous scientific evaluation methods, and to encourage policy changes based on results of randomized evaluations."

32 B. Coleman, op. cit.; A. Banerjee, et al. (2009), op. cit., and D. Karlan and J. Zinman (2009), op. cit.

33 Vol. 7, No. 1.

34 F. Buera, et al., op.cit., p. 11.

35 T. Ogden, The case for Social Investment in Microcredit, FAI blog December 2016; by contrast Khandker and Samad's non-experimental impact assessment uses long panel survey data spanning over 20 years to examine the dynamics of microcredit programmes in Bangladesh.

36 http://qualitysocialimpact.org/.

37 P. Davis, The long term Impact of Development Interventions in Rural Bangladesh, IFPRI, Project Note 2010.

38 D. Collins, et al., Portfolios of the poor, op. cit., 2009; www.bfaglobal.com.

39 N. Goldberg, *Measuring the Impact of Microfinance: Taking Stock of What We Know*, Grameen Foundation USA, 2005 and K.Odell, *Measuring the Impact of Microfinance – Taking another Look*, Grameen Foundation USA Publication, 2010, p. 6.

40 J. Bauchet, et al., op. cit., pp. 20–23.

41 Duvendack et al, op. cit., p. 4.

42 C. van Rooyen, R. Stewart, T.de Wet, The impact of microfinance in sub-Saharan Africa: a systematic review of the evidence, *World Development*, vol. 40, No. 11, 2012, pp. 2249–2262.

43 C. van Rooyen, et al, op. cit., p. 2253–6.

44 C. van Rooyen, et al., op. cit., p. 2257.

45 F.J. Buera, J. Kaboski, and Y. Shin, Taking Stock of the Evidence on Micro-Financial Interventions, NBER Working Paper No. 22674, September 2016.

46 A.M. Goetz and R.S. Gupta, *Who takes the Credit? Gender, Power and Control over Loan Use in Rural Credit Programs in Bangladesh*, IDC Sussex, 1994.

47 See, for example, CGAP, Ford Foundation and SPTF, Poverty Targeting and Measurement Tools in Microfinance: Progress out of Poverty Index (PPI) and the Poverty Assessment Tool (PAT), 2010.

48 Microsave, Client Drop-outs From East African Microfinance Institutions, Kampala, May 1999.

12 What next?

In 1997, CGAP estimated that the loan portfolios handled by all MFIs would grow to $90 billion by 2015.[1] It turns out that the loan portfolios of just of the MFIs reporting to the MIX Market was $102 billion in 2016.[2] Similarly the number of clients was anticipated to grow from 13 million in 1997 to 100 million by 2005.[3] By 2005, the actual number of clients reached was 113 million and 132 million clients in 2016.[4] The large majority of MFIs (80) operate profitably.[5] There have been more than 12 IPOs in microfinance.[6] MFIs attract $80 billion in investments. At the same time, the microfinance sector has maintained its focus on the poor, reflected in a "median average loan balance well below 30% of GNI per head."[7]

This is not bad for a strategy that continues to be criticised for having lost its sense of direction. There are reasons to be satisfied about what has been achieved. Still, financial exclusion is pervasive in many parts of the world. Two billion adults remain without an account.[8] According to the 2015 FINDEX survey, almost 40% of the adult population worldwide has no account with a financial institution (bank, microfinance institution and others). This applies to 42% of adult women, 54% of young adults (15–24 years of age) and 44% of adults living in rural areas.

Even with a significant increase in account ownership, a substantial part of transactions in poor countries continues to be handled informally. 42% of the surveyed individuals borrowed money, but only 10% from a financial institution, with the other 32% from family, friends, the moneylender, savings clubs, etc. Similarly, 56% of respondents declare to save regularly, but only 27% save with a financial institution. Improved access to accounts does not seem to have generally translated into broader usage of the services offered by financial institutions. Somehow products and services do not seem to be designed in ways that really respond to clients' needs.[9]

What next? 123

By 2030, the Sustainable Development Goals (SDGs) are supposed to be reached: will microfinance have played a role? Even if the term "microfinance" may have gone out of fashion,[10] what about the practice of microfinance, the double bottom line? Looking at the focus of recent research, it would appear that there has been a shift away from microfinance to a broader agenda of financial inclusion; but does that mean that the practice of microfinance would disappear, as demonstrated by dedicated microfinance institutions, banks, mobile network operators and others? Just as in the 19th century there were savings and credit cooperatives and municipal savings banks doing what we would call today "microfinance," so it is quite conceivable that the practice will continue, with or without the label.

In fact, it is more probable that microfinance continues as a distinct field even beyond 2020 and 2030 because the demand for small-scale, uncollateralised, convenient and affordable financial services[11] will still be there. This is at least for the following three reasons: insufficient social safety nets and social security systems, increases in migration and self-employment and application of digital finance technology.

At present, the **social security** coverage in many parts of the world is dramatically low: some 71% of the world's population has no or only partial access to comprehensive social protection systems.[12] Currently, only 16.9% of older people in sub-Saharan Africa receive an old age pension. In the absence of health, accident, old age and unemployment insurance, low-income households will have trouble withstanding income shocks. Up to now they turned primarily to informal sources. It is not likely that social security will cover all active populations in low income countries by 2030.

Migration and labour mobility – domestic and international – is likely to increase in the coming two decades with large cohorts of secondary and tertiary education graduates entering the labour market. They have few choices: stay in the country and improvise with some form of precarious self-employment or migrate. Jobs in the private sector at home are hard to come by and recruitment for government jobs is often frozen. In either scenario, there will be an increase in the demand for services – financial and non-financial – that up to now microfinance institutions have partly responded to: remittances and their transformation into financial services for the families staying behind and microloans and other services for survival start-ups in continued informality.

Digital finance will further drive down transaction costs of payments, remittances and other financial services that lend themselves to be linked to e-wallets. According to the UN, 8.6% of women-headed

124 What next?

households in Kenya were lifted out of poverty because of mobile money.[13] For the first time in history, it is conceivable that "a majority of people in a majority of places, including low-income countries, will have access to modern electronic payment services."[14] There were 3.2 billion internet users at the end of 2015, of whom two million were in developing countries. At the same time, it is estimated that two billion people worldwide do not own a mobile phone and 60% have no internet access. Africa in particular is still far from having a full coverage of mobile accounts (Figure 12.1)[15].

Of course, theoretically there can be microfinance without microfinance institutions. Money transfer organisations already started to encroach into the space of small-scale financial services as well as banks, not to speak of shops, gas stations, and other actors of agent banking. But alert MFIs take advantage of the efficiency boosts made possible by technology. The costs to the clients should come down without affecting the financial self-sufficiency of the MFI.

Technology is not a panacea to alleviate financial market failures. In 2016, 69% of mobile accounts were unused or dormant according to the GSMA,[16] not better than the dormancy rate of traditional bank accounts. Downtime problems,[17] unsuitable interfaces, risks of data privacy, fraud

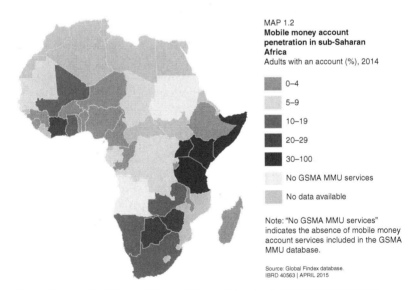

Figure 12.1 Mobile money account penetration in sub-Saharan Africa.

and cyber-insecurity explain the hesitation of millions of poor clients to embrace digital finance, especially the one billion illiterate.

It has been argued that microfinance is likely to be suffocated in future by **government** interventions. In the past, governments have adopted measures that brought about the near-demise of an entire microfinance sector, deliberately or inadvertently,[18] but in all instances the industry recovered in the end. As long as MFIs organise themselves in associations and speak with one voice to regulatory agencies, then they have a chance to survive.

Some say that **impact investing** could displace microfinance as *the* prominent, distinct double bottom line in finance. Impact investing aims at generating measurable social and environmental impact alongside a financial return. It extends the double bottom line to SME finance, agriculture, housing, education, etc. Still, it is microfinance that figures most prominently in the portfolios of impact investment funds. In 2013, it made up three-fourths of total impact investing assets under management (Table 12.1)[19].

Impact investing has adopted the metrics, methods and measurement concepts of developed by the microfinance industry. Merging into a larger investment universe does not mean the end of microfinance, rather its replication on an enlarged agenda. Microfinance thus continues to inspire other finance and investment approaches with its capacity to manage very small-scale transactions efficiently ("capillarity"), its client proximity ("last mile" distribution), voluntary codes of conducts (client protection principles), its openness to constant questioning and evaluations and its commitment to social performance.

Whether government interventionism, encroachment by other service providers or competition from similar business models, having survived three decades of growth, crises and transformations, most

Table 12.1 Microfinance in impact investment portfolios

Sector	AuM	% of AuM
Microfinance	6,400,000,000	72.1
SME finance	1,300,000,000	14.6
Agriculture	585,000,000	6.6
Housing	100,000,000	1.1
Education	17,000,000	0.2
Environment	216,000,000	2.4
Cross-sector	263,000,000	3.0
Total	**8,881,000,000**	**100**

126 *What next?*

microfinance institutions are now robust and confident enough to manage these external challenges. For microfinance practitioners, nine of the top ten risks are "internal" according to the 2017 Banana Skin Survey.

The good news is that as long as it remains committed to the double bottom line microfinance can open doors for low-income households to housing, water, health, education, transport and renewable energy. These "adjacencies" make microfinance relevant[20] also in future, against the backdrop of the 2030 Sustainable Development Goals. The term "microfinance" may fade away, but the practice of social enterprises specialised in small-scale finance will not.

Notes

1 CGAP Focus Note 3, 1995.
2 Baromètre de la Microfinance 2016.
3 The Microcredit Summit Campaign, The MCS Report, Washington, 1997.
4 State of the Microcredit Summit Report 2006.
5 Lehigh University, Microfinance – Revolution or Footnote – The future of microfinance over the next 10 years, Conference at Lehigh University March 2017, Report, p. 5.
6 Lehigh U, op.cit., p. 9.
7 Lehigh U, op. cit., p. 9.
8 A. Demirguc-Kunt, L. Klapper, D. Singer, and P. Van Oudheusden, The Global Findex Database 2014: Measuring Financial Inclusion around the World, Policy Research Working Paper 7255, World Bank, Washington, DC, 2015.
9 A. Demirguc-Kunt, L. Klapper, and D. Singer, Financial Inclusion and Inclusive Growth – A Review of Recent Empirical Evidence, Development Research Group, Finance and Private Sector Development Team, April 2017, WPS 8040, p. 19.
10 The current CGAP website does not mention "microfinance" once. The term "microfinance institutions" is replaced by "financial service provider."
11 CGAP, Vision of the Future: Financial Inclusion 2025, Focus Note 117, June 2017.
12 ILO, World Social Protection Report 2017, Geneva, p. 6.
13 T. Suri and W. Jack, The long run poverty and gender impacts of mobile money, *Science*, vol. 354, December 2016.
14 CGAP, Scenarios for Branchless Banking 2020, Focus Note 57, November 2009, p. 25.
15 A. Demirguc-Kunt and L. Klapper, L. etc. (April 2017), op. cit., p. 6.
16 UNSGSA 2017 Annual Report, p. 6.
17 UNSGSA, op.cit., p. 8.
18 Not all crises can be blamed on government: the crises in Morocco, Bosnia and Cambodia were rather the result of unmanaged growth in the portfolios of too many MFIs competing in the same small market.

What next? 127

19 CGAP Brief, Where Do Impact Investing and Microfinance Meet? June 2013, p. 2. Put into perspective: impact investing and – even more so – microfinance represent only a tiny percentage of the total estimated global investments (Symbiotics presentation at UNIGE Summer School 2014 "Investing in Microfinance").

20 www.fhi360.org/sites/default/files/media/documents/resource-id-adjacency-map.pdf. "Microfinance is ...a scalable sustainable business model to engage the poor in the market economy in a non-exploitative way... creating well-run institutions where none existed, while treating people with respect" (Lehigh U, op. cit., p. 8).

References

Websites

www.acledabank.com.kh/
www.amkcambodia.com/kh
www.almajmoua.org/FinancialServices.aspx
www.apsfdsenegal.com
www.credit-suisse.com/corporate/en/responsibility/economy-society/focus-themes/microfinance.html
www.csfi.org/financial-inclusion-banana-skins
www.cgap.org
www.eiu.com/landing/Global-Microscope
www.fiecouncil.com/about-us/
www.forbes.com/2007/12/20/microfinance-philanthropy-credit-biz
www.thegiin.org/assets/IRIS.pdf
www.stateofthecampaign.org/data-reported/
www.kiva.org
www.themix.org/mixmarket
www.mftransparency.org
www.microcapital.org
www.nobelprize.org/nobel prizes/peace/laureates/2006
www.yearofmicrocredit.org/
www.jointokyo.org/mfdl/readings/PoorMoney.pdf
www.microcapital.org/about
www.oecd.org/finance/financial-education/financial-education.htm
www.povertytools.org/
www.progressoutofpoverty.org
www.sptf.info/universal-standards-for-spm/universal-standards
www.smartcampaign.org/about/smart-microfinance-and-the-client-protection-principles
www.torontocentre.org
www.trickleup.org/graduation-approach/
www.worldbank.org/en/programs/globalfindex
www.worldfooddayusa.org/Object
www.un.org/sustainabledevelopment/development-agenda

130 *References*

Publications

Akerlof, G.A., The market for 'Lemons': quality uncertainty and the market mechanism, *Quarterly Journal of Economics*, 1970, 84 (3): pp. 488–500

Alamgir, D.A.H., Review of Current Interventions for Hard-core Poor in Bangladesh and How to Reach Them with Financial Services, Paper presented at the Credit Development Forum Workshop on Dropout Features, Extending Outreach and How to Reach the Hard-core Poor, BIDS, Dhaka, 1997

Armendariz, B. and Morduch, J., *The Economics of Microfinance*, 2nd edition, MIT Press, 2010

Armendariz, B. and Szafarz, A., On Mission Drift in MFIs, p. 341 in The Handbook of Microfinance, Singapore, 2011

Aryeetey, E., The Complementary Role of Informal Financial Institutions in the Retailing of Credit: Evaluation of Innovative Approaches, Regional Symposium on Savings and Credit for Development, Abidjan, April 1992

Aryeetey, E. and Gockel, F., Mobilizing Domestic Resources for Capital Formation in Ghana – the role of informal financial sectors. AERC Research Papers 3, Nairobi, August 1991

Balkenhol, B. (ed), *Microfinance and Public Policy*, Palgrave MacMillan and ILO, 2007

Balkenhol, B. and Schütte, H., Collateral, Collateral Law and Collateral Substitutes, Social Finance Program, Working Paper 26, ILO, Geneva, 2001

Banerjee, A.V. and Duflo, E., The economic lives of the poor. *Journal of Economic Perspectives*, 2007, 21 (1): pp. 141–168

Banerjee, A.V. et al., *The Miracle of Microfinance? Evidence from a Randomized Evaluation*, J-PAL and MIT, 2010

Baquero, G., Hamadi, M. and Heinen, A., Competition, Loan Rates and Information Dispersion in Microcredit Markets, ESMT Working Papers 12-02, Berlin, 2012

Bardhan, P., Research on Poverty and Development – 20 Years after "Redistribution with Growth," World Bank Annual Conference, 1995

Bauchet, J. and Dalal, A., Randomized experiments in microfinance, *Microfinance Insights*, 2009, 12: pp. 27–28

Bauchet, J. et al., Latest Findings from Randomized Evaluations of Microfinance, Access to Finance Forum No. 2, (CGAP, FAI, IPA, ALPAL), 2011

Bedecarrats, F. and Lapenu, C., Assessing microfinance: striking the balance between social utility and financial performance, in: J.P. Gueyie, R. Manos and J. Yaron (eds.), *Microfinance in Developing Countries – Issues, Policies and Performance Evaluation*, Palgrave McMillan, 2013

Bennett, L., *The Necessity – and the Dangers – of Combining Social and Financial Intermediation to reach the Poor*, Brookings Institution, Washington, 1994

Bennett, L. et al., Ownership and sustainability – Lessons on group-based financial services from South Asia, *Journal of International Development*, 1996, 8 (2): pp. 271–288

Berenbach, S. and Churchill, C., Regulation and Supervision of Microfinance Institutions: Experience from Latin America, Asia and Africa, Occasional Paper No. 1, Microfinance Network, Washington, DC, 1997

References 131

Berenbach, S. and Guzman, D., The Solidarity Group Experience, GEMINI Working Paper 31, June 1992

Besley, T. and Coate, S., Group lending, repayment incentives and social collateral, *Journal of Development Economics*, 1995, 46: pp. 1–18

Biosca, O. et al., Microfinance Non-Financial Services: A Key for Poverty Alleviation? Lessons from Mexico, October 2011, U Sheffield, Sheffield Economic Research Paper Series, SERP Number: 2011021

BIS (Bank for International Settlement), Basel Committee on Banking Supervision, Microfinance activities and the Core Principles for Effective Banking Supervision, February 2010

Bose, P., Formal-informal sector interaction in rural credit markets, *Journal of Development Economics*, 1998, 56: pp. 265–280

Bouman, F.J.A., Indigenous savings and credit societies in the Third World: A message? *Savings and Development Nr.* 1977, 4: pp. 181–218

Bouman, F.J.A., ROSCA and ASCRA – Beyond the Financial Landscape, Conference paper presented in Wageningen (November 1992)

Bouman, F.J.A., *Small, Short, and Unsecured – Informal Rural Finance in India*, New Delhi, OUP, 1989

Bouman, F.J.A. and Hospes, O., *Financial Landscapes Reconstructed – The Fine Art of Mapping Development*, Westview Press, 1984, pp. 179–271

Buera, F.J., Kaboski, J. and Shin, Y., Taking Stock of the Evidence on Micro-Financial Interventions, NBER Working Paper No. 22674, September 2016

Caplan, L., Multiplication of social ties – The strategy of credit transactions in East Nepal, *Economic Development and Cultural Change*, July 1972, 20 (4): pp. 691–702

Carlton, A., Manndorff, H., Obara, A., Reiter, W. and Rhyne, E., *Microfinance in Uganda, Austrian Ministry of Foreign Affairs*, Department for Development Cooperation, Vienna, December 2001

CGAP, Andhra Pradesh 2010: Global Implications of the Crisis in Indian Microfinance, Focus Note 67, November 2010

CGAP, Are Microcredit Interest Rates Excessive? Brief, February 2009

CGAP, Are We Overestimating Demand for Microloans? Brief, April 2008

CGAP, *Building Inclusive Financial Systems: Donor Guidelines on Good Practice in Microfinance*, Washington, 2004

CGAP, Commercialization and Mission Drift – The Transformation of Microfinance in Latin America, Occasional Paper 5, 2001

CGAP, Competition and Microcredit Interest rates, Focus Note 33, February 2006

CGAP, Consensus Guidelines of selected financial Terms, Ratios and Adjustments for Microfinance, 2003

CGAP, Development Finance Institutions and Financial Inclusion: From Institution-Building to Market Development, Focus Note 105, March 2017

CGAP, Financial Institutions with a Double Bottom Line – Implications for the future of Microfinance, Occasional Papers 8, July 2004

CGAP, A Guide to Regulation and Supervision of Microfinance – Consensus Guidelines, 2012

132   References

CGAP, Linking Microfinance and Safety Programs to include the Poorest, CGAP Focus Note 21, May 2001

CGAP, Measuring Results of Microfinance Institutions – Minimum Indicators That Donors and Investors Should Track – A Technical Guide, 2009

CGAP, Microfinance Consensus Guidelines – Definitions of Selected Financial Terms, Ratios and Adjustments for Microfinance, 2003

CGAP, Microfinance, Grants and Non-financial Responses to Poverty Reduction: Where Does Microcredit Fit In? Focus Note 20, December 2002

CGAP, Microcredit Interest Rates and Their Determinants, Access to Finance Forum, June 2013

CGAP, Microfinance Poverty Assessment Tool, Technical Tools Series No. 5, September 2003

CGAP, A New Look at Microfinance Apexes, Focus Note 80, June 2012

CGAP, The New Moneylenders: Are the Poor Being Exploited by High Microcredit Interest Rates? Occasional Paper 15, February 2009

CGAP, Presentation "Branchless Banking 101," Sarah Rotman, March 29, 2012

CGAP, Reaching the Poorest – Lessons from the Graduation Model, Focus Note 69, March 2011

CGAP, Regulating and Supervision of MFIs – Stabilizing A New Financial Market, Focus Note no.4, August 1996

CGAP, Regulation and Supervision of Microfinance, Donor Brief 12, 2003

CGAP, The Role of Governments in Microfinance, Donor Brief No. 19, June 2004

CGAP, The Rush to Regulate: Legal Frameworks for Microfinance, Occasional Papers 4, 2000

CGAP, Scenarios for Branchless Banking 2020, Focus Note 57, November 2009

CGAP, Taking Stock - Recent Trends in International Funding for Financial Inclusion, Brief, December 2016

CGAP, Vision of the Future: Financial Inclusion 2025, Focus Note 117, June 2017

CGAP, Where Do Impact Investing and Microfinance Meet? Brief, June 2013

CGAP and Symbiotics, White Paper: Microfinance Funds – 10 Years of Research and Practice, December 2016

CGAP, Ford Foundation and SPTF, Poverty Targeting and Measurement Tools in Microfinance: Progress out of Poverty Index (PPI) and the Poverty Assessment Tool (PAT), 2010

Chandavarkar, A.G., The Role of Informal Credit Markets in Support of Microbusinesses in Developing Countries, Paper presented at World Conference on Support for Microenterprises, Washington, June 1988

Chen, G. et al., Indian Microfinance Goes Public: The SKS Initial Public Offering, CGAP Focus Note 65, September 2010

Chipeta, C. and Mkandawire, M.L.C., Links between the Informal and Formal/Semiformal Financial Sectors in Malawi, AERC Research Paper, Nairobi, November 1992

Christen, R., Rhyne, E., Vogel, R.C., Maximizing the Outreach of Microenterprise Finance: The Emerging Lessons of Successful Programs, USAID, 1995

References   133

Churchill, C., Insurance for the poor: definitions and innovations, in: B. Armendariz and M. Labie (eds.), *Handbook of Microfinance*, World Scientific Publishing, 2011

Coleman, B., The impact of group lending in Northeast Thailand, *Journal of Development Economics*, 1999, 60: pp. 105–141

Collins, D., Morduch, J., Rutherford, S. and Ruthven, O., Portfolios of the Poor: How the World's Poor Live on $2 a Day, Princeton UP, 2009

Copestake, J., Goldberg, N. and Karlan, D., Randomized control trials are the best way to measure impact of microfinance programmes and improve microfinance product designs. *Enterprise Development and Microfinance*, 2009, 20 (3): pp. 167–176

Cull, R., Demirguç-Kunt, A. and Morduch, J., Financial performance and outreach: a global analysis of leading micro-banks, *Economic Journal, Royal Economic Society*, 2007, 117 (517): pp. F107–F133

Cull R., Demirguc-Kunt A. and Morduch, J., The Microfinance Business Model – Enduring Subsidy and Modest Profit, Policy Research Working Paper 7786, World Bank Development Research Group, August 2016

Cull, R., Demirguç-Kunt, A. and Morduch, J., Microfinance Trade-offs – Regulation, Competition, and Financing, Policy Research Working Paper 5086, The World Bank Development Research Group, Finance and Private Sector Team, October 2009

Darko, F.A., Is There a Mission Drift in Microfinance? Some New Empirical Evidence from Uganda, University of Kent School of Economics Discussion Papers, March 2016, KDPE 1603

Demirguc-Kunt, A., Klapper, L. and Singer, D., Financial Inclusion and Inclusive Growth – A Review of Recent Empirical Evidence, Development Research Group, Finance and Private Sector Development Team, April 2017, WPS 8040

Demirguc-Kunt, A., Klapper, L., Singer, D. and Van Oudheusden, P., The Global Findex Database 2014: Measuring Financial Inclusion around the World, Policy Research Working Paper 7255, World Bank, 2015

de Soto, H., *The Mystery of Capital: Why Capitalism Triumphs in the West and Fails Everywhere Else*, Basic Books, 2000

Dichter, T., *Hype and Hope: The Worrisome State of the Microcredit Movement*, Blog on Microfinance Gateway, CGAP, 2006

Dikki, A.C., Impact of non-financial services of Microfinance Banks (MFBs) on the performance of women entrepreneurs in Nigeria, *European Journal of Business and Management*, 2014, 6 (34): pp. 158–163

Dominicé, R., Microfinance Investments, Symbiotics, 2012

Donovan, K., *Mobile Money for Financial Inclusion, Information and Communications for Development*, World Bank, 2012

Dowla, A., Political interference in microfinance, *Enterprise Development and Microfinance*, December 2015, 26 (4): pp. 358–373

Drexler, A., Fischer, G. and Schoar, A., Keeping it simple: Financial literacy and rules of thumb, *American Economic Journal: Applied Economics*, 2014, 6 (2): pp. 1–31

134 References

Duflo, E., Banerjee, A., Glennerster, R., Kinnan, C.G., The Miracle of Microfinance? Evidence from a Randomized Evaluation, Working Paper 18950, NBER, May 2013

Dunn, E. and Arbuckle, G., Microcredit and microenterprise performance: impact evidence from Peru, *SED*, 2001, 12 (4): pp. 22–33

Duvendack, M., Palmer-Jones, R., Copestake, J.G., Hooper, L., Loke, Y. and Rao, N., What is the Evidence of the Impact of Microfinance on the Well-being of Poor People? Research Report. London: EPPI-Centre, Social Science Research Unit, Institute of Education, University of London 2011

Engels, P., *Mission Drift in Microfinance, The Influence of Institutional and Country Risk Indicators on the Trade-off between the Financial and Social Performance of Microfinance Institutions*, Tilburg University, October 2009

European Microfinance Platform, The Role of Investors in Promoting Social Performance in Microfinance, Number 1, June 2008

Fernando, N., Micro Success Story? Transformation of NGOs into Regulated Financial Institutions, ADB, June 2004

Ferro Luzzi, G. and Weber, S., Measuring the performance of MFIs: an application of factor analysis, in: B. Balkenhol (ed.), *Microfinance and Public Policy*, Palgrave MacMillan and ILO, 2007

Fleisig, H., The Power of Collateral, Viewpoint Note 43, World Bank, April 1995

Fleisig, H., The Right to Borrow, Viewpoint Note 44, World Bank, April 1995

Fleisig, H., Secured Transactions: The Power of Collateral, Finance and Development, June 1996

Fleisig, H. et al., Legal Restrictions on Security Interests Limit Access to Credit in Bolivia, *The International Lawyer*, 1997, 31 (1): pp. 65–110

Flückiger, Y. and Vassiliev, A., Efficiency in microfinance institutions: an application of data envelopment analysis to MFIs in Peru, in: B. Balkenhol (ed), *Microfinance and Public Policy*, Palgrave Macmillan and ILO, 2007

Ford Foundation, CGAP, EU and SPTF, Poverty Targeting and Measurement Tools in Microfinance, October 2010

Fox, L. and Sohnesen, T., Household Enterprises in Sub-Saharan Africa - Why They Matter for Growth, Jobs, and Livelihoods, Policy Research Working Paper 6184, World Bank, August 2012

Gentil, D. et al., Banquiers ambulants et Opération 71 au Togo et Bénin, Working Paper 1, Social Finance Program, ILO, Geneva 1992

Germinidis, D. et al., Financial Systems and Development: What Role for the Formal and Informal Financial Sectors? OECD Development Centre, 1991

Gershman, J. and Morduch, J., Credit is Not a Right, Financial Access Initiative Research Framing Note, April 2011

Ghate, P.B., Interaction between the formal and informal financial sectors: the Asian experience, *World Development*, 1992, 20 (6): pp. 859–872

Gine, X. and Karlan, D., Group versus individual liability: short and long term evidence from Philippine microcredit lending groups, *Journal of Development Economics*, 2014, (107): pp. 65–83

Goetz, A.M. and Gupta, R.S., *Who takes the Credit? Gender, Power and Control over Loan Use in Rural Credit Programs in Bangladesh*, IDC Sussex, 1994

References 135

Goldberg, M. and Hunte, P., Financial Services for the Poor: Lessons on Group-based Models from Five South NGOs, World Bank Asia Technical Department, 1995

Gonzalez, A., Is Microfinance Growing Too Fast? MIX Data Brief No. 5, June 2010

Goodman, P., International Investment Funds – Mobilizing Investors towards Microfinance, ADA Luxembourg, November 2003

Gray, B., Gash, M., Reeves, S., Crookston, M., Microfinance – a sustainable platform for non-financial services, *Progress in Economics Research*, 2011, 20: pp. 163–182

GSMA, State of the Industry Report on Mobile Money, Decade Edition: 2006–2016, 2017

GSMA, 2015-State of the Industry Report Mobile Money, 2016

Gutiérrez-Nieto, B., Serrano-Cinca, C. and Mar Molinero, C., Social efficiency in microfinance institutions, *Journal of Operational Research Society*, 2009, 60: pp. 104–119

Hermes, N., Lensink, R. and Meesters, A., Outreach and Efficiency of Microfinance Institutions, Centre for International Banking, Insurance and Finance (CIBIF), University of Groningen, 2007

Honohan, P., Financial Sector Policy and the Poor – Selected Findings and Issues, World Bank Working Paper 43, 2004

Hudon, M. and Traca, D., Subsidies and Sustainability in Microfinance, ULB CEB Working Paper 06–20, Brussels, October 2006

IFC, Why Banks in Emerging Markets Are Increasingly Providing Non-financial Services to Small and Medium Enterprises, Washington, DC, 2012

ILO, World Social Protection Report 2017, Geneva

IPA, Beyond the Classroom – Evidence on New Directions in Financial Education, Financial Inclusion Program Brief, IPA, January 2017

Javoy, E. and Rozas, D., MIMOSA 2.0: Mapping the (micro) credit cycle, 2015

Kar, A.K., Measuring competition in microfinance markets: a new approach, *International Review of Applied Economics*, 2016, 30 (4): pp. 423–440

Kar, A.K. and Swain, R.B., *Competition, Performance and Portfolio Quality in Microfinance Markets – A Study using Global Panel Data*, U Helsinki, 2014

Karlan, D. and Goldberg, N., *The Impact of Microfinance: A Review of Methodological Issues*, FAI, 2006

Karlan, D. and Valdivia, M., Teaching entrepreneurship: impact of business training on microfinance clients and institutions, *The Review of Economics and Statistics*, May 2011, 93 (2): pp. 510–527

Karlan, D. and Zinman, J., Expanding Microenterprise Credit Access: Using Randomized Supply Decisions to Estimate the Impacts in Manila, 2010

Krauss, A., Lontzek, L., Meyer, J. and Frommelt, M., Lack of Access or Crowded Markets? Towards a Better Understanding of Microfinance Market Penetration, University of Zürich, Department for Banking and Finance, Center for Microfinance, Working Paper 23, August 2012

Ledgerwood, J., Microfinance Handbook – An Institutional and Financial Perspective, World Bank, Sustainable Banking with the Poor, 1999

136 References

Ledgerwood, J. and White, V., Transforming Microfinance Institutions – Providing Full Financial Services to the Poor, World Bank, 2006

Lehigh University, Microfinance – Revolution or Footnote – The Future of Microfinance over the Next Ten Years, Conference at Lehigh University, March 2017

Lelart, M., Bibliographie sur l'Epargne et le Crédit informels, Notes de Recherche No. 90/11 UREF/AUPELF, 1990

Lelart, M., Les Tontines et le Financement de l'Entreprise Informelle, Notes de Recherche 18, UREF-AUPELF, 1991

Lensink, R., Mersland, R., Hong Vu, Thong and Zamore, St., Do microfinance institutions benefit from integrating financial and nonfinancial services? *Applied Economics*, 2018, 50 (21): pp. 2386–2401

Llanto, G., Balkenhol, B. and Zulfikli, M., Breaking Barriers to Formal Credit – Asian Experiences on collateral substitutes, APRACA/ILO/SDC, Bangkok, 1996

Lhériau, L., *Précis de la Réglementation de la Microfinance*, AFD, Paris, 2009

Maimbo, S.M. and Henriquez Gallegos, C.A., Interest Rate Caps around the World – Still Popular, but a Blunt Instrument, Finance and Markets Global Practice Group, Policy Research Working Paper 7070, WB, October 2014

Mc Kernan, M.S., The impact of microcredit programs on self employment profits: do non-credit program aspects matter? *Review of Economics and Statistics*, February 2002, 84 (1): p. 109

McIntosh, C. and Wydick, B., Competition and microfinance, *Journal of Development Economics*, 2005, 78: pp. 271–298

Mersland, R. and Strom, R.O., Microfinance mission drift? *World Development*, January 2010, 38 (1): pp. 28–36

Mersland, R. and Urgeghe, L., Performance and international investments in microfinance institutions in "International Debt Financing and Performance of Microfinance Institutions," *Strategic Change: Briefings in Entrepreneurial Finance*, 2013, 22 (1–2): pp. 17–29

Meyer, R.L., The demand for flexible microfinance products: lessons from Bangladesh, *Journal of International Development*, April 2002, 14 (3): pp. 351–368

Meyer, J., Krauss, A. and Nelung, C., Measuring and Aggregating Social Performance of Microfinance Investment Vehicles, Center for Microfinance, Department of Banking and Finance, University of Zürich, 2016

Microcredit Summit Campaign, State of the Microcredit Summit Reports, Washington, 1997

Microrate, The State of Microfinance Investment, 2011

MIX Market, The 2008 MIX Global 100 Composite Rankings of Microfinance Institutions, A report from the Microfinance Information Exchange, Inc. (MIX), December, 2008

Morduch, J., The role of subsidies in microfinance: evidence from the Grameen Bank, *Journal of Development Economics*, 1999, 60: pp. 230–246

Morduch, J., Smart subsidy for sustainable microfinance, ADB Finance for the Poor, December 2005, 6 (4): pp. 1–7

Navajas, S. et al., Microcredit and the poorest of the poor: theory and evidence from Bolivia, *World Development*, 2000, 28 (2): pp. 333–346

References 137

Odell, K., Measuring the Impact of Microfinance – Taking another Look, Grameen Foundation USA, 2000, 28 (2): pp. 333–346

OECD/INFE International Survey of Core Competencies of Adult Financial Literacy, Paris, 2016

Olivares-Polanco, F., *Commercializing Microfinance and Deepening Outreach? Empirical Evidence from Latin America*, U Pittsburgh, 2003

Otero, M., *A Question of Impact, Solidarity Group Programs and their Approach to Evaluation*, PACT Publication, September 1989

Paxton, J., Depth of Outreach and its Relation to the Sustainability of Microfinance Institutions, *Savings and Development*, 2002, XXVI (1): pp. 69–86

Paxton, J. et al., Modelling group loan repayment behaviour: new insights from Burkina Faso, *Economic Development and Cultural Change*, 2000, 48 (3): pp. 639–655

Pine, D., The Microfinance Sector in Bangladesh: Innovation or Stagnation, BA Thesis in Banking and Finance, Center for Microfinance, University of Zürich, 2010

Porteous, D., Collins, D. and Abrams, J., Prudential Regulation in Microfinance, Financial Access Initiative Policy Framing Note, 2010

Prahalad, C.K., *The Fortune at the Bottom of the Pyramid – Eradicating Poverty Through Profits*, Wharton School Publishing, 2004

Puri, S. and van Rooij, P., Microfinance and Poverty – A Comparative Assessment of the Impact of Conditional Micro-grants and Micro-credit in Nepal and Uganda, ILO, Social Finance Program, ILO, Geneva, unpublished working paper

Rahman, A. and Wahid, A.N.M., The Grameen Bank and the changing Patron-Client relationship in Bangladesh, *Journal of Contemporary Asia*, 1992, 22 (3): pp. 303–321

Rating Initiative, Rating Guide, Volume 1: The Microfinance Institutional Rating, October 2012

Roodman, D., *Due Diligence – An Impertinent Inquiry into Microfinance*, Center for Global Development, Washington, 2012

Roodman, D. and Morduch, J., *The Impact of Microcredit on the Poor in Bangladesh: Revisiting the Evidence*, FAI and NYU Wagner, 2009

Rosenberg, R., Reflections on the Compartamos Initial Public Offering: A Case Study on Microfinance Interest Rates and Profits, CGAP Focus Note 42, June 2007

Rosenberg, R., Gaul, S., Ford, W., Tomilova, O., Microcredit Interest Rates and Their Determinants, CGAP, Access to Finance Forum, Reports by CGAP and its Partners No. 7, June 2013

Roth, J., Informal Micro-Finance Schemes: The Case of Funeral Insurance in South Africa, Social Finance Programme, Working Paper 22, ILO, 2000

Rozas, D. and Sinha, S., Avoiding a microfinance bubble in India: is self-regulation the answer? *Microfinance Focus*, 10 Jan 2010

Rutherford, S., The Economics of Poverty: How Poor People Manage Their Money, Corporation for Enterprise Development, Washington, 2002

Rutherford, S., *The Poor and Their Money*, DFID, Oxford University Press, 1999

138 References

Seibel, H.D., Mainstreaming informal financial institutions, *Journal of Developmental Entrepreneurship*, April 2001, 6 (1): pp. 83–95

Seibel, H.D., History matters in microfinance, *Small Enterprise Development*, June 2003, 14 (2): pp. 10–12

Sen, A., The Political Economy of Targeting, World Bank Conference on Public Expenditures and the Poor: Incidence and Targeting, Washington, June 1992

Sinha, S., Bangladesh Microfinance Review, Dhaka, 2011

Spaggiari, L. Guidelines on Outcomes Management for Investors, European Dialogue, No. 10, October 2016

Spence, M., Job market signalling, *Quarterly Journal of Economics*, 1973, 87 (3): pp. 355–374

Staschen, S., Regulatory Requirements for Microfinance, GTZ, Division 41 Economic Development and Employment Promotion, Eschborn, 2003

Steinwand, D., The Alchemy of Microfinance, Berlin, 2001

Stiglitz, J.E. and Weiss, A., Asymmetric information in credit markets and its implication for macroeconomics, *Oxford Economic Papers*, 1992, 44: pp. 694–724

Stiglitz, J.E. and Weiss, A., Credit rationing in markets with imperfect information, *American Economic Review*, June 1981, 71 (3): pp. 393–410

Suri, T. and Jack, W., The long run poverty and gender impacts of mobile money, *Science*, December 2016, 354: pp. 1288–1292

Symbiotics/CGAP, Microfinance Funds 10 Years, 2016

Symbiotics, 2017 MIV Survey – Market Data and Peer Group Analysis, September 2017

Timberg, T.A. and Aiyar, C.V., Informal credit markets in India, *Economic Development and Cultural Change*, October 1984, 33 (1): pp. 43–59

UNSGSA (UN Secretary General's Special Advocate for Inclusive Finance for Development), Annual Report 2017

Van Rooyen, R., Stewart, R. and de Wet, T., The impact of microfinance in sub-Saharan Africa: a systematic review of the evidence, *World Development*, 2012, 40 (11): pp. 2249–2262

Von Pischke, J.D., Finance at the Frontier, World Bank, Washington, 1991

Von Stauffenberg, D. and Rozas, D., Role reversal revisited – are public development institutions still crowding out private investment in Microfinance? *Microrate*, January 2011

Waterfield, C., Transparency in Microfinance – the Client Perspective, UMM/ Frankfurt School, Frankfurt, July 2012

Webster, L., *The Informal Sector and Microfinance Institutions in West Africa*, World Bank, 1995

Woller, G., The Promise and Peril of Microfinance Commercialization, *Small Enterprise Development*, 2002, 13 (4): pp. 12–21

Woller, G. and Chemonics for USAID, Proposal for a Social Performance Measurement Framework in Microfinance: The Six Aspects of Outreach, Micro REPORT #26, July 2005

Woolcock, M.J., Learning from failures in microfinance – What unsuccessful cases tell us about how group-based programs work, *American Journal of Economics and Sociology*, January 1999, 58 (1): pp. 34–35

References 139

World Bank, Targeting the Poor, Development Brief, number 9, February 1993

World Bank and IMF, Financial Sector Assessment – A Handbook, Chapter 7: Rural and Microfinance Institutions: Regulatory and Supervisory Issues, 2005

Wright, D., In-Country Donor Coordination, CGAP Focus Note 19, April 2001

Wright, G., *Microfinance Systems: Designing Quality Financial Services for the Poor*, The University Press Limited, 2000

Wright, G., Understanding and Assessing the Demand for Microfinance, Microsave, Paris, June 2005

WWB, Microfinance Equity Fund, New York, 2008

WWB, What do Microfinance Customers Value? New York, 2002

Xu, L. and Zia, B., Financial Literacy around the World – An Overview of the Evidence with Practical Suggestions for the Way Forward, World Bank, Development Research Group, Finance and Private Sector Development Team, June 2012, WPS6107

Yaqub, S., Empowered to default? Evidence from BRAC's micro-credit programmes, *Small Enterprise Development*, 1995, 6: pp. 4–13

Yaron, J., Assessing Development Financial Institutions: A Public Interest Analysis, World Bank Discussion Paper 174, Washington, 1992

Zeller, M., Sources and Terms of Credit for the Rural Poor in the Gambia, African Review of Money, Finance and Banking, 1, 1994

Index

absorption capacity: household-enterprises 18

ACLEDA in Cambodia: financial and social goals 46; transformation from NGO into micro-bank 54–55

adverse selection: transparency in contracts 9

Africa: average interest rate on credit lines 101; debt financing 100; mobile banking 25; poverty targeting strategies 32

agent–principal relationships: transparency in contracts 9

Al Majmoua in Lebanon: clients 19; products 22

APEX funds 101–102

assets: informal 36; quality regulations 94

average cost per withdrawal transactions 25

Bancosol: transformation from NGO into micro-bank 55–56

Bangladesh: market concentration 79

the bottom of the pyramid 2

branchless banking 25

capacity building measures of public policies 90–92

capital adequacy: regulating 93–94

"Caregiver Hospital Cash Policy" programme 21

CGAP (Consultative Group to Assist the Poor): Graduation Program 16

challenges 2

Client Protection Principles 95–96

clients 21; centricity 64; expectations for MFIs 47; financial education 91; individual micro-entrepreneurs 4; MFI typical 19; organising into groups 34–35; protection principles 66; regulations for protection 95–96; targeting 31–34; women organised in solidarity groups 4

collateral substitution 35–38; informal assets 36; legal enforcement 38; marketable value 38; performance in enforcing repayment 38; property registries 36–37

commercial banks: appraising default risks of informal potential clients 8–9; interest rates comparison to MFIs and informal financial sector 11

commercialisation 2; MFI performance 52–53

competition: effects on mission drift 83–85; household-enterprises 17; markets 79–82; public policies 98–100

concentration: market 78–79

conditional cash grants 28

conditional micro-grants 27–28

consumer loans 21–22

contracts: commercial bank failures 8–9; commitments 65; interlinked in informal finance 11; lacking transparency causes 9

cooperative MFIs: features 45; liabilities structure 23; profitability

142 *Index*

and outreach 46; self-employed poor women in India 22
costs: determining products and services 24; group *versus* individual lending cost implications 34–35; public policy 89
cross-subsidisation of social programmes 73–74
crowding out 67–68
Cull, R.: avoiding mission drift 57

debt investors 64
degree of formalisation target 31–32
demand for financing: flexibility 16–17; household-enterprises 17–19; living situations 16; poverty levels 16; products offered 23
deposit products 24
destitute: conditional micro-grants 28
DFIs (development finance institutions): crowding out 67–68
digital finance 123–125
distortion of markets 72
diversifying: financial transactions with several agents 11–12; funds from initially agreed uses in household-enterprises 19; household-enterprises into other income generating activities 18
donors *see* subsidies
double bottom line 3
dropouts 15–16

education impact 112
efficiency: avoiding mission drift 57; Latin American MFIs 73; public policies 89–90; subsidies 72
eligibility criteria: MFIs 45
enterprise non-financial services 28
Equity Bank in Kenya 15
equity investors 64
European Microfinance Platform: Guidelines on Outcomes Management for Investors 67
evolution of microfinance 4
external challenges: digital finance 123–125; impact investing 125; migration 123; public policies 125; social security coverage 123

features: MFIs 45; microfinance 5
financial attitude 91
financial diaries 115
financial education: clients 91
financial inclusion 122
financial knowledge 91
financial performance of MFIs 49–50; by charter type 47–48; commercialisation 52–53; mission drift 56–58; peer group metric 58–60; transformation 53–56
financial services: non-financial services combinations 38–39
financial transactions: simplistic view 7; transaction costs 8
fiscal measures of MFIs 102
fixed income investments 65
flexibility: MFIs 15–16
food grain donation conditional micro-grant 28
food security microfinance 21
Ford Foundation Graduation Program 16
FSS (financial self-sufficiency): MFI financial performance 49
funding: informal economy 10; instrument of public policy 100–102; intertwined consumption and investment funding needs 17–19
future of microfinance 123; demand 123; digital finance 123–125; impact investing 125; migration 123; public policies 125; social security coverage 123

government funding 100–102
government intervention *see* public policies
government-owned and -run retail institutions 101–102
Graduation Program 16
Grameen Bank: microcredit to women organised in solidarity groups 4; Nobel Peace prize 1; subsidies 73
grants 27–28
gross yield: competition effect 81
group lending 34–35
Guidelines on Outcomes Management for Investors 67

Index 143

health impact 112
Hermes, N.: avoiding mission drift 57
historic microfinance institutions 4
household consumption stabilisation
  conditional cash grants 28
household-enterprises: absorption
  capacity 18; competition by
  individuals operating in the
  same line of business 17; defined
  17; diversification into other
  income generating activities 18;
  diversifying financial transactions
  with services agents 11–12;
  diversion of funds from initially
  agreed uses 19; intertwined
  consumption and investment
  funding needs 17–19; life-cycle
  events effects 19; non-financial
  services 26–27; poverty impact
  measurement difficulties 116–117;
  risk aversion 18
household non-financial services 26
housing microloans 21
hybrid insurance and savings
  products 21

IGVGD (Income Generation for
  Vulnerable Groups Development)
  programme 28; cross-subsidisation
  of 73–74
impact investing 124–125
impact of microfinance: definition
  109–110
impact on poverty 110–111;
  critical factors 116–118;
  distorted outcomes by group
  constitution 113; financial diaries
  115; household-enterprises
  complications 116–117;
  meta- evaluations 115–116;
  Millennium Development Goals
  by UN 111; QiIP 115; RCTs
  113–114; well-being improvements
  111–112
income: generating activities target
  31; impact 112
indebted farmers and microfinance
  institutions clash in India 2
indicators: social performance 50–51
indirect subsidies 70

individuals: *versus* group lending
  cost implications 34–35;
  micro-entrepreneur clients 4
informal assets 36
informal economies: absorption
  capacity 18; among individuals
  financial transactions 12;
  competition by individuals
  operating in same line of business
  17; diversification into other income
  generating activities 18; diversion of
  funds from initially agreed uses 19;
  household-enterprises diversifying
  financial transactions with services
  agents 11–12; individual financial
  transactions 12; informal finance
  funding 10; information asymmetry
  10; intertwined consumption and
  investment funding needs 17–19;
  lifecycle events effects 19; mutual
  financial transactions 12; risk
  aversion 19
informal finance: funding informal
  economy 10; household-enterprises
  diversifying financial transactions
  with services agents 11–12; interest
  comparison to banks and MFIs
  11; interlinked contracts 11; MFI
  advantages over 13; shortcomings
  11–12
information asymmetry: informal
  economy 10; transparency in
  contracts 9
insider lending: regulating 94
institutions *see* MFIs
instruments of public policies:
  capacity building 90–92; funding
  100–102; regulation 92–100
insufficient social security
  coverage 123
interest rates: Africa average 101;
  banks, MFIs, and informal
  financial sector comparison
  11; ceiling regulation 96–98;
  components of interest yields 82;
  evolution 81; global yield trends
  79–80
interlinked contracts 11
intertwined funding needs of
  household-enterprise 17–19

144   *Index*

investors: client centricity 64; client protection principles 64; contractual commitments 65; crowding out 67–68; debt investors 64; effects on double bottom line 67; equity 64; fixed income investments 65; Guidelines on Outcomes Management for Investors 67; MFI attractability 62; MFI social performance 68; performance commitments of MFIs 65–67; relationship between types of investors and types of investment funds 63; social performance 66; subsidies comparison 70

joint liability groups 34–35; as collateral substitute 36

Kashf in Pakistan: microfinancing schooling and education 21

Latin American MFI efficiency and profitability 73
legal forms determining liabilities structure 23
legality: collateral substitution 38
lending: group *versus* individual cost implications 34–35; joint liability groups 34–35; methodology effects on mission drift 57
liabilities structure determined by legal form 23
life-cycle events: effects on household-enterprises 19
liquidity: regulating 94
living situations: demand for finance 16
loan products 23
LSMS (Living Standard Measurement Survey) 16

marketable value: collateral substitution 40
markets: competition 79–82; concentration 78–79; differentials with prices charged by comparable service providers 80; distortion 72; failures 8–10; global interest yield

trends 80; mission drift 83–85; penetration 78; saturation 82–83; size 77–78
maternal health programme 21
media: shaping perceptions 2
Mersland, R.: avoiding mission drift 57
message of microfinance 1
meta-evaluations of poverty impact 115–116
methods: collateral substitution 35–38; financial and non-financial services combinations 38–39; joint liability groups 34–35; targeting 31–34
MFIs: advantages over informal finance 13; attractability to investors 62; client categories 19; client expectations 47; commercialisation 52—53; digital finance 123–125; dropouts 15–16; effects of regulations 95; eligibility criteria 45; features 45; financial performance 47–50; fiscal measures 102; flexibility 15–16; future demand 123; growth 122; historic microfinance 4; household-enterprises clients 17; interest rate ceiling effects 97–98; interest rates comparison to banks and informal financial sector 11; joint liability groups 34–35; legal forms determining liabilities structure 23; mission drift 56–58; MIVs effects on double bottom line 67; pattern of refinancing 23; peer group performance metric 58–60; performance commitments from MIVs 65–67; profitability and outreach 3, 46; quality 48; resources driving products 23–24; slack performance from subsidies 71–72; social performance 47, 50–51, 68; transformation 53–56; types 44–48; worldwide number of 43–44
MHFC in India: micro housing loans 21
micro-banks: NGOs transforming into 54–56

Index 145

microfinance banks: features 45; profitability and outreach 46
micro housing loans 21
micro-insurance 21, 24
migration: demand for MFIs 123
Millennium Development Goals 111
minimum capital requirements: regulating 93
mission drift: competition effects 83–85; MFIs 56–58
MIVs (Microfinance Investment Vehicles) 63; client centricity 64; client protection principles 64; contractual commitments 65; crowding out 67–68; debt investors 64; effects on double bottom line 67; equity investors 64; fixed income investments 65; Guidelines on Outcomes Management for Investors 67; MFI social performance 68; performance commitments of MFIs 65–67; relationship between types of investors and types of investment funds 63; social performance 68
MIX Market: listing of MFIs 43–44; social performance indicators 51
M-Kesho 25
mobile banking M-Pesa example 25
modern microfinance: precursors 4
monetary policies: interest rate ceilings 96–98
money transfers 25
moral hazard: government-owned and -run retail institutions 101–102; subsidies 72; transparency in contracts 9
Morduch. J., smart subsidies 74–75
motorcycle bankers in West Africa 10
M-Pesa example 25
multiple donors 73

NBFIs (non-banking financial institutions): Cambodia 46; features 45; liabilities structure 23; profitability and outreach 46
NGOs (non-governmental organisations): commercialisation 53; features 45; liabilities structure 23; profitability and outreach 46;

state activism 103; transforming into micro-banks 54–56
Nobel Peace prize: Yunus and the Grameen Bank 1
non-financial services 26–27; enterprise needs or household needs 26; financial services combination 38–39

organising clients into groups 34–36
OSS (operational self-sufficiency): MFI financial performance 49
outreach *see* social performance of MFIs
over-indebtedness protection 22
ownership: regulating 94

pattern of refinancing 23
peer groups performance metric for MFIs 58–60
performance of MFIs 47–48; commercialization 52–53; financial 49–50; mission drift 56–58; peer groups metric 58–60; slack performance from subsidies 71–72; smart subsidies 74–75; social 50–51; transformation 53–56
Pocantino Declaration 95
politics: challenge 2; state activism 102–103
post-disaster situations: conditional micro-grants 30
poverty impact 110–111; critical factors 116–118; distorted outcomes by group constitution 113; financial diaries 115; household- enterprises complications 116–117; meta-evaluations 115–116; Millennium Development Goals 111; QiIP 115; RCTs 113–114; well- being improvements 111–112
poverty levels: demand for finance 16
poverty targeting 31–34; African poverty targeting strategies 32; consequences from straying from declared target markets 32–33; criticisms 35–36; degree of formalization 31–32; expenses and yields 33; income generating activities 31; individual

146 *Index*

characteristics 33; limited diversification risk 33; overlapping criteria 32; places of residence 31; tested score-cards for measurement of poverty 33
precursors to modern microfinance 4
preventing over-indebtedness 22
price dumping: government-owned and -run retail institutions 102
principal-agent relationships: transparency in contracts 9
products 21; absence of consumer loans 21–22; cost determinant 24; demand driven 23; deposit 24; examples 23–24; resources determinant 23–24; SDGs 21; technology determinant 25
profitability: institutions 3; Latin American MFIs 73; MFIs 46, 49
property registries: collateral substitution 36–37
protecting clients: MIVs 64; regulations 95–96
public policies: asset quality 94; benefits 92–93; capacity building 90–92; capital adequacy 93–94; client protection 95–96; competition 98–100; costs 89, 93; effects 95; efficiency 89–90; funding 100–102; future of microfinance 125; insider lending 94; interest rate ceilings 96–98; justification of government intervention 88; minimal capital requirements 93; ownership 94; regulation 92–100; reserves and liquidity 94; respecting MFI business models 89; risk concentration 94; state activism 102–103

QiIP (Qualitative Impact Protocol) 115
quality: assets 94; MFIs 48

rapid portfolio growth 83
RCTs (randomized control trials): poverty impact 113–114
regulations: asset quality 94; benefits 92–93; capital adequacy 93–94; client protection 95–96; competition 98–100; costs 89, 93;

effects 95; future of microfinance 125; insider lending 94; interest rate ceilings 96–98; minimum capital requirements 93; ownership 94; reserves and liquidity 94; risk concentration 94
repayment: collateral substitution 38
reserves: regulating 94
resources: driving product offerings 23–24
retail subsidies 70
risk aversion: household-enterprises 18
risk concentration: regulating 94

Sathapana in Cambodia: products 22
saturation: markets 82–83
savings products 22
schooling and education microloans 21
Schreiner, M.: outreach framework 50
SDGs (Sustainable Development Goals) 21; 2030 SDGs 126; access to finance 88; attainment 123; financial self-sufficiency 50; microfinance products 21; mission drift 57
SDI (Subsidy Dependence Index) 72
selecting clients *see* targeting
services: cost determinant 24; demand driven 23; financial and non-financial combination 38–39; grants 27–28; mobile banking 25; non-financial 26–27; resource determinant 23–24; technology determinant 25
SEWA Bank in India: products 22
slack performance: from subsidies 71–72
The Smart Campaign 22, 95
smart subsidies 74–75
social performance of MFIs 46–47, 50–51; commercialization 52–53; cross-subsidization 73–74; mission drift 56–58; MIV investments 70; peer group metric 58–60; Social Performance Task Force and MIX Market indicators 51; transformation 53–56; USAID outreach framework 50
social performance of MIVs 68–69
Social Performance Task Force: Guidelines on Outcomes

Management for Investors 67; social performance indicators 51

social security coverage insufficiency 123

social services 26–27

state activism 102–103

State Government of Andhra Pradesh in India indebted farmers clash 2

Strom, R.O.: avoiding mission drift 57

subsidies: cross-subsidization of social programmes 73–74; efficiency 72; indirect 70; investments comparison 70; moral hazard 72; multiple donors 73; normal MFIs 74; retail 70; SDI 72; slack performance 71–72; smart 74–75; vindicating financial autonomy 71; world-wide amounts of 71

supervision *see* regulations

Sustainable Development Goals *see* SDGs

targeting 31–34; African poverty targeting strategies 32; consequences from straying from declared target markets 32–33; criticisms 33–34; degree of formalisation 31–32; expenses and yields 33; income generating activities 31; individual characteristics 31; limited diversification risk 33; overlapping criteria 32; places of residence 31; tested score-cards for measurement of poverty 33

technology: determining products and services 25; digital finance 123–125

tontines 11

transaction costs 8

transformation of MFIs 53–56; ACLEDA from NGO into micro-bank 54–55; Bancosol from NGO into micro-bank 55–56; effects on double bottom line 54; motivations 54

transparency: causes of lacking 9; complete 7–8

Trickle-Up conditional cash grants 28

twin indicators of profitability (OSS and FSS): MFIs 49

types of MFIs 44–48

ultra-poor: reaching out to 16

University of Zürich's Centre for Microfinance MIV social performance measurement methodology 66

UN Millennium Development Goals 111

USAID outreach framework 50

welfare improvements 4

West African motorcycle bankers 10

Woller, G.: outreach framework 50

women: IGVGD 28; maternal health program 23; organized in solidarity groups clients 4; targeting 31; tontines 11; WWB Microfinance Equity Fund 65–66

World Bank LSMS (Living Standard Measurement Survey) 16

WWB (Women's World Banking): maternal health programme 21; Microfinance Equity Fund 65–66

Yunus and the Grameen Bank: Nobel Peace prize 1

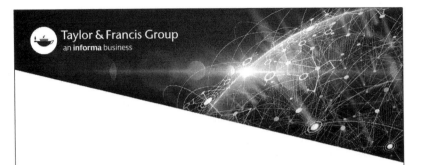

Taylor & Francis eBooks

www.taylorfrancis.com

A single destination for eBooks from Taylor & Francis with increased functionality and an improved user experience to meet the needs of our customers.

90,000+ eBooks of award-winning academic content in Humanities, Social Science, Science, Technology, Engineering, and Medical written by a global network of editors and authors.

TAYLOR & FRANCIS EBOOKS OFFERS:

A streamlined experience for our library customers

A single point of discovery for all of our eBook content

Improved search and discovery of content at both book and chapter level

REQUEST A FREE TRIAL
support@taylorfrancis.com